Making Financial Globalization

Making Financial Globalization

How Firms Shape International Regulatory Cooperation

CLARA PARK

OXFORD
UNIVERSITY PRESS

Oxford University Press is a department of the University of Oxford.
It furthers the University's objective of excellence in research, scholarship,
and education by publishing worldwide. Oxford is a registered trade mark of
Oxford University Press in the UK and in certain other countries.

Published in the United States of America by Oxford University Press
198 Madison Avenue, New York, NY 10016, United States of America.

© Oxford University Press 2025

All rights reserved. No part of this publication may be reproduced,
stored in a retrieval system, or transmitted, in any form or by any means,
without the prior permission in writing of Oxford University Press,
or as expressly permitted by law, by license or under terms agreed with
the appropriate reprographics rights organization. Inquiries concerning
reproduction outside the scope of the above should be sent to
the Rights Department, Oxford University Press, at the address above.

You must not circulate this work in any other form
and you must impose this same condition on any acquirer

Library of Congress Cataloging-in-Publication Data
Names: Park, Clara (Bora Clara), author.
Title: Making financial globalization : how firms shape international
regulatory cooperation / Clara Park.
Description: New York, NY : Oxford University Press, [2024] |
Includes bibliographical references and index.
Identifiers: LCCN 2024022583 | ISBN 9780197761823 (paperback) |
ISBN 9780197761816 (hardback) | ISBN 9780197761847 (epub)
Subjects: LCSH: International finance. | International economic relations. |
International trade. | Financial services industry–International cooperation.
Classification: LCC HG3881 .P2948 2024 | DDC 332.042—dc23/eng/20240607
LC record available at https://lccn.loc.gov/2024022583

DOI: 10.1093/oso/9780197761816.001.0001

Integrated Books International, United States of America

Contents

List of Figures	vii
List of Tables	ix
Acknowledgments	xi

1. Puzzle of Financial Globalization	1
1.1 Financial Globalization: A Brief History	3
1.1.1 Trade in Financial Services	5
1.2 Argument in Brief	6
1.2.1 Theoretical Contributions	10
1.3 Research Design	13
1.4 Plan of the Book	15
2. A Theory of Financial Globalization	17
2.1 Preferences in Financial Globalization	18
2.1.1 Preferences of Governments in Financial Globalization	20
2.1.2 Preferences of Multinational Financial Corporations	23
2.2 A Theory of Financial Globalization	24
2.3 Mechanism for Multilateral Lobbying	31
2.4 Quiet Politics and Financial Globalization	38
2.5 Alternative Explanations	40
2.5.1 International Explanations	40
2.5.2 Domestic Explanations	41
2.5.3 Reverse Causality	43
2.6 Scope and Limitations	43
2.7 Conclusion	44
3. Financial Linkage and Financial Globalization	47
3.1 Measuring Financial Linkage	48
3.2 Impact of Financial Linkage on Financial Firms' International Expansion Strategies	51
3.2.1 Citi's International Expansion Strategies	55
3.2.2 Financial Linkage and Citi's Expansion in Ghana	57
3.3 A Quantitative Analysis of Financial Linkage and Financial Globalization	59
3.3.1 Results	62
3.3.2 Optimal Matching Analysis	64
3.3.3 Robustness Checks	66
3.4 Conclusion	69

vi CONTENTS

4. Fragmented Liberalization in the Financial Industry 70
    4.1 Why Does Government Ownership in the Financial Industry Matter? 73
    4.2 Types of Entry Barriers in the Financial Market 75
    4.3 Analysis: Government Ownership and Financial Trade Liberalization 79
        4.3.1 Number of Restrictions 81
        4.3.2 Severity-Weighted Entry Restrictions 81
        4.3.3 Distribution of Entry Restrictions 82
        4.3.4 Model and Data 83
        4.3.5 Robustness Tests 87
    4.4 Conclusion 87

5. De Jure Liberalization: Lowering Entry Regulations 89
    5.1 Mechanisms 90
        5.1.1 Creating a New International Regime 91
        5.1.2 Creating an International Depository of Financial Regulations 93
    5.2 Did Countries Change Their Financial Regulations? 97
        5.2.1 Latin America 98
        5.2.2 East Asia 102
    5.3 Regulatory Developments in the US and China 107
        5.3.1 Changing Financial Regulations in the US 108
        5.3.2 Opening the Chinese Financial Market 111
    5.4 Conclusion 123

6. De Facto Liberalization: Cross-Border Financial Flows 126
    6.1 Increase of Foreign Banks around the World 127
        6.1.1 Mergers and Acquisitions 129
    6.2 Analysis of FSA Membership and Financial Flows 130
        6.2.1 Research Design and Data 132
    6.3 Results 134
        6.3.1 Trade in Financial Services 134
        6.3.2 FDI 135
        6.3.3 Portfolio Investment 136
    6.4 Discussion 138

7. Conclusion 140
    7.1 Firm-Driven International Economic Negotiations 144

Bibliography 149
Index 163

List of Figures

1.1 Changed fortunes in government and foreign ownership of banking assets in 136 countries, 1988–2016 ... 2

1.2 Global financial flows increased sharply around the turn of the century ... 3

1.3 Financial services exports and imports, 1980–2013 ... 13

2.1 Government control moderates the effect of financial linkage on the number of conditions imposed in liberalization schedules ... 23

2.2 Process of financial globalization ... 25

2.3 Industry coalitions designed to increase firms' bargaining leverage ... 28

2.4 Members of the Financial Leaders Group ... 34

2.5 Members of the Financial Leaders Working Group ... 35

3.1 Financial linkage pushes firms and governments ... 48

3.2 Distribution of financial linkage in 63 countries ... 50

3.3 Five industries with the highest financial linkage in the US ... 50

3.4 Financial linkage by GDP quintile ... 51

3.5 Stages of banking business expansion ... 52

3.6 Financial linkage around the world ... 61

3.7 Probability of signing the FSA as a function of financial linkage ... 62

3.8 Average treatment effects at varying split quantiles ... 65

3.9 Covariate balance plot of raw and matched sample ... 65

4.1 Total number of financial trade restrictions, by country ... 71

4.2 Excerpt of the US FSA schedule ... 80

4.3 Distribution of entry restrictions ... 82

4.4 Effect of government ownership on entry barriers in finance ... 86

5.1 Liberalization of regulations on foreign entry and strengthened independent regulation in banking, 1997–2007 ... 98

5.2 Excerpt of China's FSA schedule ... 117

6.1 Changes in capital flows before and after joining the FSA ... 138

List of Tables

2.1 Predicted Liberalization as Function of Financial Linkage and Government Control in the Financial Industry	22
2.2 Alternative Explanations	40
3.1 Citi's Investment by Country, Amount, and Industry, 1995–1997	56
3.2 Citi's 15 Largest Invested Firms, 1995–1997	56
3.3 Marginal Effect of Financial Linkage on Probability of FSA Signing	63
3.4 Average Treatment Effect on the Treated (ATT) of High Financial Linkage on the Probability of Signing the FSA	66
3.5 Robustness Checks	67
4.1 Regression of Number of Restrictions and Severity-Weighted Restrictions on Government Ownership	85
4.2 Robustness Checks	87
5.1 Domestic Finance Legislation Listed in Countries' FSA Schedules	95
5.2 Domestic Finance Legislation Listed in Countries' FSA Schedules, Continued	96
5.3 Regulatory Changes Related to Foreign Entry and Liberalization in Latin America, 1997–2007	99
5.4 Regulatory Changes to Regulators' Independence in Latin America, 1997–2007	103
5.5 Regulatory Changes to Foreign Entry and Liberalization in East Asia, 1997–2007	104
5.6 Regulatory Changes to Regulators' Independence in East Asia, 1997–2007	106
6.1 Asian Countries with the Most Foreign Banks	127
6.2 Foreign Banks with the Largest Presence in Asia	128
6.3 Latin American Countries with the Most Foreign Banks, 1998–1999	129
6.4 Foreign Banks with the Largest Presence in Latin America	130
6.5 Major Mergers of Financial Firms	131
6.6 Effect of Joining the FSA on the Level of Import of Trade in Financial and Insurance Services	134

X LIST OF TABLES

6.7 Effect of Joining the FSA on Changes in Total FDI (Inflows and Outflows) 136

6.8 Effect of Joining the FSA on the Incidence of Positive Portfolio Equity Inflows 137

Acknowledgments

It was summer of 2008, when everything seemed to spin out of control. I was working at a Wall Street investment bank in midtown New York City during the global financial crisis. Banks that existed for over a hundred years disappeared in a blink of an eye, and the whole system seemed to be on the verge of explosion. I wanted to understand the systemic impact of the financial market, why and how financial markets across countries became so interconnected, and how some banks became "too big to fail." I thus began the journey to understand international finance and international relations.

I thank my advisors at the University of California, Berkeley: Vinnie Aggarwal, Steve Vogel, Alison Post, and Noam Yuchtman, without whom I would not have been able to do this research. Vinnie is the best mentor anyone could hope for, and I only wish to be a mentor like him to my students. Steve provided invaluable support and advice and helped arrange my research in Japan. Alison and Noam challenged me to broaden my audience. I also thank Kevin O'Brien, Peter Lorentzen, and Gerard Roland, for their insightful teaching of the Chinese economy.

I had a wonderful time during my postdoctoral fellowship at Duke University. Giovanni Zanalda and Yan Li at the Asian/Pacific Studies Institute supported my international fieldwork to Asia and Europe. Tim Büthe, Eddy Malesky, Margaret McKean, Pablo Beramendi, Kyle Beardsley, and Peter Feaver also supported my research at Duke.

I also thank my colleagues at the University of Colorado Boulder, including David Bearce, Andy Baker, Adrian Shin, David Brown, Carew Boulding, and Chinnu Parinandi, who provided comments and advice. I also thank scholars who gave invaluable feedback on my research, including Dennis Quinn, Jeff Frieden, David Steinberg, Tom Pepinsky, Judy Goldstein, and Cameron Ballard-Rosa, among others. I thank my research assistants, Chris Hussey from Berkeley and Rhys Ogg and Anushka Kathait from Colorado for their excellent assistance.

I thank all my interviewers in Washington, DC; Geneva; Brussels; and Tokyo—I met some phenomenal public servants as well as industry representatives, lobbyists, and practitioners, who took time out of their busy

xii ACKNOWLEDGMENTS

schedule to talk to me about their experiences and perspectives on international trade negotiations. In fact, the main argument of the book developed out of my first interview in Washington, DC, and the rest of the interviews opened my eyes to different sides of the exciting and hardworking world of international negotiations. The librarians at the National Archives, Library of Congress, and the WTO were immensely helpful.

I also thank Layna Mosley, Nita Rudra, and Mike Tomz, who have attended my book workshop. Their insightful comments and encouragements have improved this manuscript. I also thank the two anonymous reviewers and my editor at Oxford University Press, David McBride, as well as Emily Benitez and the production team at OUP. I also thank Kelley Friel for her excellent copyediting. Lastly, my deepest gratitude is to my parents and I dedicate this book to them.

1

Puzzle of Financial Globalization

The world has become financially globalized. Multinational banks are now ubiquitous from Argentina to Zimbabwe: people can walk into the branches of Citi, HSBC, and Barclays in the United States as well as in Brazil, China, and Ghana, and use their credit cards around the world. American Insurance Group (AIG) brings in a third of its revenue from its foreign operations,[1] and investment banks such as Morgan Stanley and Goldman Sachs underwrite securities and advise on mergers and acquisitions in every corner of the world.

However, finance has traditionally been local—and state controlled. Given its political and economic importance, governments all over the world have directly or indirectly controlled the financial industry,[2] especially outside the US.[3] Latin American countries, such as Argentina, Brazil, Chile, and Mexico, have oscillated between financial protection and liberalization as populist leaders have come and gone.[4] East Asian countries such as China, Japan, and Korea have traditionally had a heavy state presence in the financial sector.[5] Even some developed countries, such as France[6] and

---

[1] AIG 2019, Form-10K (Annual Report pursuant to Section 13 or 15(d) of the Securities Exchange Act of 1934), p. 6.

[2] Caprio et al. 2010.

[3] While the United States does not have a large state-owned banking sector, it has traditionally guaranteed or backed mortgage-backed securities since the "issued or guaranteed 95% or more of all MBS [mortgage-backed securities] issued annually since 2008" through government-sponsored entities such as Fannie Mae (Federal National Mortgage Association), Freddie Mae (Federal Home Loan Mortgage Corporation), and Ginnie Mae (Government National Mortgage Association). See Government Accounting Office 2019, p. 2.

[4] Frieden 1991a; Brooks 2004; Menaldo and Yoo 2015.

[5] See Haggard and Maxfield 1996; Cho 1999; US Department of State 2019.

[6] France has long had heavy state ownership of the financial industry; it nationalized the three largest banks (BNP, Crédit Lyonnais, and Société Générale) between 1945 and 1987, and founded and controls Crédit Agricole. The French government also currently owns the sixth-largest bank, La Banque Postale (postal bank). For details on France's historical nationalization of its banks, see Central Intelligence Agency 1982.

Making Financial Globalization: How Firms Shape International Regulatory Cooperation. Clara Park, Oxford University Press. © Oxford University Press 2025. DOI: 10.1093/oso/9780197761816.003.0001

2 MAKING FINANCIAL GLOBALIZATION

Germany,[7] have maintained a large government presence in the financial industry.[8]

Governments kept out multinational financial corporations (MFCs), which are often more technologically advanced and efficient than local financial firms, because they feared losing control over their financial market to foreigners.[9] To maintain control, governments erected entry barriers against foreign financial firms, such as foreign ownership restrictions. For example, many countries did not allow 100% foreign-owned financial firms in their markets; they required a joint venture with a local financial firm (50% ownership) or minority ownership (less than 50%). Some of them also had higher minimum capital requirements for foreign financial firms than for domestic financial firms.

Starting in the late 1990s, however, governments around the world started to lower entry barriers in their markets, and MFCs expanded their operations abroad. Figure 1.1 illustrates the share of government ownership and

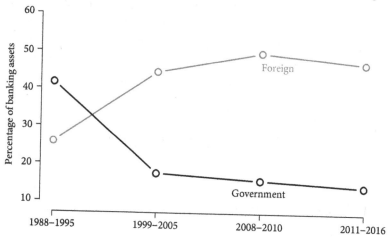

Figure 1.1 Changed fortunes in government and foreign ownership of banking assets in 136 countries, 1988–2016. Share of banking assets indicates whether a government or foreign firm controls more than 50% of a bank's assets. For foreign ownership, the 1988–1995 data is from Claessens et al. (2001); the rest is from the World Bank Regulations Survey (Barth et al. 2001). The 1995 data on government ownership is from La Porta et al. (2002), and the rest is from Anginer et al. (2019).

---

[7] The public sector accounts for 46.4% of Germany's total banking assets, which comprises savings banks, or *Sparkassen* (13.8%); state banks, or *Landesbanken* (21%); and special purpose banks, or *Förderbanken* (11.6%). See Hau and Thum 2009. The German state maintained a 51% share of Postbank, which is now a retail arm of Deutsche Bank (as of 2019). See Forbes 2019.

[8] For more on state ownership in developed countries, see Verdier 2000; Epstein 2017; Naqvi et al. 2018; Mertens and Thiemann 2018; OECD 2018.

[9] Claessens et al. 2001; Rajan and Zingales 2003; Micco et al. 2007; Pepinsky 2013.

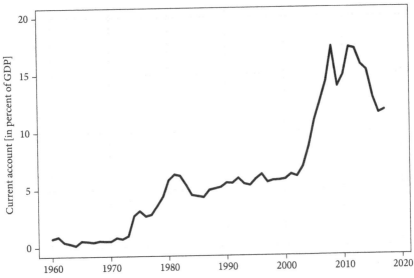

Figure 1.2 Global financial flows increased sharply around the turn of the century. Financial flows as reflected in the ratio of current account balance to GDP. The figure indicates a sharp increase around 2001. Current account (mean absolute value) data is from IMF (2020). GDP data is from the World Bank (2020).

foreign ownership in 136 countries. It shows that government ownership fell from 42% in 1988–1995 to 18% in 1999–2005, and foreign ownership doubled from 26% to 47% during the same period.[10] The increase in foreign ownership also coincided with the tripling of cross-border financial flows around the turn of the century (Figure 1.2). What explains financial globalization around the turn of the century?

1.1 Financial Globalization: A Brief History

Financial globalization, which the International Monetary Fund (IMF) defines as "increasing global linkages created through cross-border financial flows," significantly expanded beyond developed countries in the nineteenth century.[11] During colonial times, financial firms followed their corporate clients—colonial traders—when they went to the New World to get spices, tea, or raw materials. MFCs followed their clients to new markets in Asia,

---

[10] These findings are based on an unbalanced panel of 136 countries; however, the pattern is similar for a balanced panel of 80 countries.
[11] Bordo et al. 1999; Kose et al. 2004.

4 MAKING FINANCIAL GLOBALIZATION

Africa, and Latin America to help them with cross-border financial transactions. In the second half of the twentieth century, international economic cooperation and technological developments led to increases in cross-border capital flows.[12] The IMF-led capital account liberalization facilitated international capital flows around the world.[13] Trade also expanded during this period. The General Agreement on Tariffs and Trade (GATT) lowered tariffs on physical goods: average world tariff levels fell from 22% to a low point of 1.6% between 1947 and 2016.[14] However, services (e.g., financial, telecommunications, and legal services) had been considered "untradable" on the basis that it was impossible to separate their production from their consumption, although they grew as a share of national GDP.[15]

Starting in the 1970s, technological developments enabled services to be provided via mail or phone—and later, the Internet. This enabled service providers, such as financial service providers, to expand to new markets. However, they faced behind-the-border barriers, such as entry barriers and discriminatory regulations, in host countries. This increased the uncertainty and transaction costs of foreign entry for service providers. The GATT, by design, is a framework of tariffs and cannot govern nontariff barriers.[16] Thus, there was a growing demand for an international framework that would address both behind-the-border domestic regulations on market access and nondiscrimination in trade in services.

Recognizing this gap in governance, firms engaged in a multilateral lobbying campaign to create an international framework for trade in services in the 1980s. Years of negotiations resulted in the General Agreement on Trade in Services (GATS), which formed a part of the newly created World Trade Organization (WTO), in 1995. The GATS covers all services, including legal, education, telecommunications, and financial services, and obligates

---

[12] The end of World War II heralded the founding of multiple new international economic institutions—the IMF to govern the international monetary system, the General Agreement on Tariffs and Trade (GATT) to administer international trade, and the International Bank for Reconstruction and Development (IBRD, which became the lending arm of the World Bank Group) to manage development.

[13] Eichengreen (2019) identifies a U-shaped pattern of international capital mobility: expansion before World War I, contraction during the interwar period, and further expansion in the late twentieth century. For a discussion of variation in financial liberalization, see Quinn 2003.

[14] See Bown and Irwin 2016 and World Bank WTI Database.

[15] By the mid-1980s, private service industries accounted for over 40% of US GDP (Gross Domestic Product by Industry for 1987–2000, US Bureau of Economic Analysis, Chart 2). See also Sauvant 1993.

[16] Trade liberalization in goods involves tariff schedules that list the stepwise reduction of tariffs each year until they reach zero, in most cases. Contemporary trade disputes have gone beyond quantitative restrictions to nontariff barriers like subsidies and antidumping measures.

PUZZLE OF FINANCIAL GLOBALIZATION 5

countries to grant market access and non-discriminatory treatment to foreign service providers. However, one of the most contentious negotiations in GATS was trade in financial services, due to the strategic nature of the financial industry.

1.1.1 Trade in Financial Services

Trade liberalization in financial services focuses on removing barriers to financial service provisions that facilitate these capital flows. It is different from capital account liberalization, which focuses on removing barriers to short-term capital flows, such as equities and bonds.[17] Trade in financial services includes *commissions* on cross-border banking, insurance, and securities services, and long-term foreign direct investment (FDI) in the financial sector, such as establishing branches, subsidiaries, and wholly owned financial firms (i.e., Citibank in China and Credit Suisse in the US). For example, a financial service provider charges a commission for issuing loans, insurance products, or securities.[18] If a cross-border loan commission is 2% on a $2 million loan ($40,000), the commission would be entered into the country's current account (export/import of financial services), while the $2 million loan would be entered into the country's capital account.[19]

Trade in financial services occurs through four modes of supply: cross-border trade, consumption abroad, commercial presence, and the natural movement of persons following the GATS framework. *Cross-border trade* (mode 1) takes place when services are provided across borders—for example, if an insurance company in the Netherlands (e.g., ING) sells insurance services to residents in the US over the phone, via the Internet, or by mail. *Consumption abroad* (mode 2) occurs when a person purchases services

---

[17] Quinn and Inclan 1997; Dobson and Jacquet 1998; Mattoo 1999; Kireyev 2002.

[18] Financial services rates are determined by fees that are assessed on a flat rate (per task), fixed rate (per hour), commission (percentage), or transaction profit basis. Imagine a real estate agent charges a commission based on the house value for their services, including showing houses and negotiating offers (e.g., a 3% commission on a $300,000 house would be $9,000). See Asmundson 2011.

[19] Under the service categories in UN EBOPS 2010, financial services "may be charged for by: explicit charges, margins on buying and selling transactions, asset management costs deducted from property income receivable, in the case of asset-holding entities, and margins between the interest rate and the reference rate on loans and deposits referred to as financial intermediation services indirectly measured or FISIM" (IMF 2009, p. 172).

6 MAKING FINANCIAL GLOBALIZATION

while traveling abroad—for instance, if a US citizen travels to Italy and buys travel insurance while they are there.

One of the most contentious negotiations related to trade in financial services liberalization involved mode 3—*commercial presence* of foreign financial firms (e.g., Citibank opening a branch in Thailand or Deutsche Bank entering the US)—because it allows foreign firms to enter the market and compete directly with domestic firms. This mode also accounts for the largest share of trade in services (60%).[20] *Natural movement of persons* (mode 4) is work-related migration. For example, if a Citibank employee moves from the US to France to work for Citibank's French office, she is engaging in trade in financial services. However, many countries severely restrict this mode of supply due to the sensitive political nature of free movement of persons across borders.

1.2 Argument in Brief

The most common explanation for (financial) globalization is the external force that breaks down borders and barriers. Prior studies of market liberalization examined the international factors behind this trend, such as diffusion,[21] financial crises,[22] and power asymmetry.[23] Other studies examined domestic factors, such as regime type,[24] partisanship[25] and factor endowment,[26] for countries' decision to liberalize. While these studies explain individual countries' decisions to liberalize, they do not explain why governments around the world lowered their entry barriers and strengthened their financial regulators contemporaneously.

I argue that financial globalization occurred because firms pushed for (and shaped) the creation of a new international financial services regime, which lowered entry barriers in financial markets around the world. In 1997, a total of 102 countries, which accounted for 95% of the global

---

[20] According to the WTO, commercial presence (mode 3) accounts for 58.9% of trade in services. Cross-border trade (mode 1) is the second highest at 27.7%, consumption abroad (mode 2) accounts for 10.4%, and the presence of individuals in another country (mode 4) accounts for 2.9% (in 2017, see WTO 2019).

[21] Simmons and Elkins 2004.

[22] Haggard and Maxfield 1996; Martinez-Diaz 2009; Pepinsky 2012.

[23] Przeworski and Vreeland 2000; Drezner 2001; Mukherjee and Singer 2010.

[24] Quinn 2000; Milner and Mukherjee 2009; Jensen et al. 2012; Menaldo and Yoo 2015; Steinberg et al. 2018.

[25] Pinto and Pinto 2008.   [26] Frieden 1991b.

trade in financial services, joined the WTO's Financial Services Agreement (FSA), which was the first (and remains the only) multilateral agreement on trade in financial services liberalization.[27] These countries included financial leaders, such as the US, UK, EU, and Japan, but also many countries without comparative advantages in financial services, such as Egypt, Gabon, and Kenya. The signatories agreed to open their markets to foreign financial firms and update their domestic regulations to reflect the new international norms of liberalization and nondiscrimination.[28]

Why did countries create this agreement to liberalize their financial markets? In contrast to the state-centric explanations for international regime creation, this study focuses on *firm-driven* regime creation for financial globalization. I argue that firms engaged in *multilateral lobbying* to create an international agreement. Firms created industry coalitions, selected an international forum (GATT/WTO) for negotiating trade in financial services liberalization, provided the language of the new regime—norms, rules, principles, and procedures—to government negotiators, and facilitated international negotiations by working with home and host governments and international organizations during the negotiations.

Historically, financial firms followed their corporate clients that expanded overseas—what the international business literature calls the "follow-the-client" hypothesis.[29] This is because financial firms provide services (banking, insurance, and securities services) that firms use to produce their outputs. When industrial firms expand overseas in search of new markets and cheaper inputs (e.g., large agriculture businesses expanding to Latin America or manufacturing plants moving to Southeast Asia), financial firms often follow their clients to provide cross-border financial services, such as international loans, insurance for goods during transit, and merger and acquisition services. For example, Citibank entered Zambia, which does not have a large financial market, to provide cross-border financial services to mining companies. It established only two offices in Zambia—one in the capital city of Lusaka and another in the mining hub of Ndola.

---

[27] See Aggarwal 1992 and Aggarwal and Ravenhill 2001 for sectoral agreements in the services sector.
[28] White House, Statement by Secretary Rubin and Ambassador Barshefsky, December 13, 1997: "The commitments encompass $17.8 trillion in global securities assets; $38 trillion in global (domestic) bank lending; and $2.2 trillion in worldwide annual insurance premiums" (USITC 1998, p. 18).
[29] Gray and Gray 1981; Nigh et al. 1986; Goldberg and Johnson 1990; Buch 2000.

8 MAKING FINANCIAL GLOBALIZATION

This is known as financial linkage, which measures an economy's financial dependence, derived from input-output linkages: how one industry's outputs are used as intermediate inputs in another industry.[30] For example, a manufacturing factory borrows money from the bank to buy land and equipment (banking services), takes out insurance to protect its products during production and transit (insurance service), and issues equity (securities services). Industry linkage is widely used in international economics and macroeconomics studies to examine the interdependence of industries in order to measure differences in productivity and the multiplier effects of economic shocks across industries.[31] International political economy (IPE) scholars have long studied the importance of cross-industry linkages in international trade negotiations and international regimes.[32] The growing literature on global value chains also explores intersectoral linkages to examine how a rise in demand for an industry's output could lead to a corresponding increase in demand in the industry's upstream and downstream industries' backward and forward linkages.[33]

However, as many firms face obstacles when expanding abroad, MFCs also found it particularly difficult to enter many markets. This is because many governments had entry barriers to protect their domestic financial markets, which are strategically and economically important to governments. Thus, MFCs had to negotiate with host governments over these entry barriers, which were often nontransparent and discriminatory. As the number of desired markets to enter increased, the bilateral transaction costs of negotiating entry increased. Thus, MFCs looked for a way to reduce entry barriers in many countries at the same time.[34]

During this time, CEOs of large MFCs—especially Citi, AIG, and American Express—learned they were facing similar entry bargaining problems around the world.[35] They had been serving on industry advisory boards to the US government on trade policy, such as the GATT, and saw how effective the international framework was in lowering tariffs on goods. Thus, they decided to create an international framework on financial services liberalization.

---

[30] Alfaro et al. 2010; Acemoglu et al. 2012; Fadinger et al. 2015.
[31] Hirschman 1958; Rodriguez-Clare 1996; Dunning and Lundan 2008; Jones 2011; Bartelme and Gorodnichenko 2015.
[32] Haas 1980; Lohmann 1997; Aggarwal 1998; Davis 2004.
[33] Alfaro et al. 2010; Acemoglu et al. 2012; Gereffi 2014; Fadinger et al. 2015; Miroudot and Cadestin 2017; Kim et al. 2019; Malesky and Milner 2021.
[34] Brainard et al. 1997; Helpman et al. 2004.   [35] Freeman 2000.

In order to create an international framework, firms engaged in multilateral lobbying. Firms were at the forefront of commercial expansion, so they were familiar with entry barriers around the world.[36] However, since the financial industry is important to many countries, MFCs assessed that it would have been difficult to gain sufficient political support for an international agreement on financial services alone. Thus, they decided to create a new framework on services, GATS, to lower behind-the-border barriers (just like the GATT lowered tariffs), and include financial services as a part of the new framework. They recruited other industries and formed coalitions across industries and countries to increase the number of stakeholders and leverage over politicians. They picked an international forum for negotiations—the GATT (later the WTO)—over the existing international financial organizations, such as the IMF or the Bank for International Settlements, for a blank canvas to create a new regime on trade in services. They created norms and principles, such as transparency, nondiscrimination, and independent regulation, and the desired level of liberalization in each country of interest, and facilitated international negotiations. It was *firms* that even coined the term "trade in services" and promoted it to government officials and the media in the early days of negotiations. Former American Express executive Harry Freeman wrote about creating the term "financial services":

> Another thing that we had to deal with very, very early on is the meaning of financial services. The first thing we did in 1979 was to coin the phrase. You will not see the term "financial services" before 1979. We did that by asking everybody in the company to talk about financial services particularly with the media, and in about two years the term financial services was part of the lexicon ... Every time they [journalists] would say the phrase "goods," I would give the clip to my office manager and say, "Write this reporter, sign my name, and say that he left out the term 'services.'" And that worked.[37]

The industry coalitions not only worked with their domestic governments[38] but also with host governments and international institutions to create a new international regime. They traveled around the world to convince governments that financial service liberalization would bring in much-needed capital and advanced financial services that would benefit their exporters, as well as technology and competition to modernize their financial industry.

---

[36] Greenberg and Cunningham 2013.   [37] Freeman 1998, p. 457.   [38] Putnam 1988.

10 MAKING FINANCIAL GLOBALIZATION

Since countries could not agree on trade in financial services liberalization during the Uruguay Round, they split off financial services from the GATS negotiations as a stand-alone sectoral agreement. After years of negotiations, the FSA was finally signed in December 1997. Countries agreed to open up their markets to FDI in the financial sector and cross-border financial services.[39]

Governments then joined this agreement and lowered entry barriers to MFCs, despite the risk of losing control in the market, so that their domestic industrial firms could access external capital and global financial services. The entry of MFCs would allow domestic industrial firms, especially exporters, to access global financial services and capital.[40] However, in order to protect their domestic financial firms during liberalization, governments embedded restrictions in their liberalization commitments to control the speed and extent of foreign entry. After joining the international agreement, countries subsequently engaged in regulatory reforms to lower domestic regulatory entry barriers in their financial markets.

In sum, while globalization seems exogenous, this book argues that firms engaged in a *multilateral lobbying* campaign to open up the global financial market. Firms organized across industries and countries to push for the creation of a new international regime in financial services and change financial regulations around the world. Governments, even those without comparative advantages in financial services, liberalized their financial markets in order to bring in external capital while maintaining control in the financial market. The lowered entry barriers around the world allowed MFCs to expand their international operations and facilitate more cross-border financial flows, leading to financial globalization.

1.2.1 Theoretical Contributions

The study's findings have three main implications for (1) our understanding of the strategic interactions of firms and governments in financial globalization, (2) firms' international political strategies in financial

---

[39] See Dobson and Jacquet 1998 for country cases of the FSA negotiations. There were four sectoral negotiations in the post–Uruguay Round: information technology, basic telecommunications, financial services, and maritime services. Telecommunications reached an international agreement, the 1996 Basic Telecommunications Agreement. See Aggarwal 1992 for more on sectoral agreements in the services sector.

[40] Aitken and Harrison 1999; Javorcik 2004; Bekaert et al. 2011; Danzman 2019.

PUZZLE OF FINANCIAL GLOBALIZATION   11

globalization, and (3) how the separate literatures on international trade
and finance can be integrated.

First, the book argues that while the literature has focused on states' role
in international organization policymaking, states are not the only actors
that create regimes. Firms now play an increasingly important role in international negotiations.[41] This book explores firms' increasing influence in
international regime *creation*. It highlights financial firms' structural power,
not only in the domestic policy sphere, but also in international organization policymaking. Moreover, it describes a new configuration of interests and institutions beyond sectoral and national boundaries—whether
(and how) political alignment can occur *across* sectors, instead of just
along sectoral lines.[42]

Second, and relatedly, my approach examines firms' international
political strategies—how they utilize international negotiations to reduce
regulatory barriers around the world. While previous studies on business
and politics have mainly focused on domestic economic policies "in isolation
from international or macro processes"[43] and firms' (passive) responses to
policies,[44] my argument traces how firms' material interests affect their
strategies to enact macro-level changes in financial globalization to actively
create international economic policy.[45] The book examines how firms utilize
all available tools domestically and internationally—engaging not only with
their home governments[46] but also directly with host governments, international organizations, and firms in other countries to create an international

---

[41] Frieden (1987) and Milner (1988b) assess how a firm's position in the global political economy
affects its preferences regarding economic policies. Malesky (2009) examines foreign investors'
influence on economic reforms. Osgood et al. (2017) evaluates the dimensions of trade agreements
and finds that preferences vary by firm, not by industry, according to their position in global
production networks. For more studies, see Jensen et al. 2015; Madeira 2016; Weymouth 2017; Kim
and Osgood 2018; Osgood 2021.

[42] The rise of intra-industry trade and global value chains has challenged traditional models of
political alignment in support of/opposition to trade policies along sectoral lines. See Markusen
1989; Melvin 1989; Francois and Hoekman 2010; Eichengreen and Gupta 2011; Marchetti and
Mavroidis 2011; Miroudot et al. 2012; Weymouth 2017; Bernard et al. 2018; Baccini et al. 2019.

[43] Lake 2009, p. 311. Also see Keohane 2009; Oatley 2011, 2017. They pointed out that some open
economy politics studies lack mechanisms that link micro-level foundations (such as individual,
group, and firm preferences) with macro-level processes. An emerging literature examines multinational corporations' influence on trade-related policies such as regulatory protection (Gulotty,
2020) and immigration policy (Peters, 2017). For more on foreign lobbying, see Gawande et al.
2006; Malesky 2009; You 2020.

[44] For prior studies on domestic politics in lobbying policy, see Schattschneider 1935; Putnam
1988; Gawande et al. 2012; De Figueiredo and Richter 2014.

[45] Katzenstein et al. 1978; Milner 1992; Cortell and Davis 1996.

[46] Grossman and Helpman 1994; Putnam 1988.

12 MAKING FINANCIAL GLOBALIZATION

liberalization regime that would enact contemporaneous domestic regulatory changes.

Lastly, this study bridges the two distinct literatures of international finance and trade, which have been examined separately up until now. Prior studies on international trade have focused largely on trade in goods liberalization,[47] while the international finance literature on capital flows examined capital account liberalization.[48] Examining trade openness and financial openness separately creates a gap in understanding the patterns of cross-border capital flows and the impact of financial development on economic growth.[49] Trade in financial services liberalization removes barriers to the cross-border provision of financial services as well as long-term FDI in the financial sector, which then facilitates short-term capital account flows. By evaluating entry barriers and FDI liberalization in the financial services industry,[50] this study bridges the literatures on international finance and trade and contributes to the literature on endogenous financial and trade openness.[51]

Trade and finance had been governed separately for almost half a century due to the institutional division between the WTO and the IMF. The FSA ended the half-century division of labor between the WTO and the IMF in global economic governance. It allowed the WTO to expand its reach into the realm of finance and has since served as the blueprint for the financial services chapter in bilateral free trade agreements.[52] Trade in services grew to account for 13% of global GDP[53] and 51% of the world's total employment.[54] Figure 1.3 displays the total global trade in financial services (exports and imports) from 1980 to 2013, which spans the period before and after FSA implementation in 1999. It illustrates that the rate of change for trade in services changed significantly after the FSA's implementation.

---

[47] Milner 1988a; Melitz 2003; Kim 2017; Osgood 2018.

[48] Quinn 2003; Mosley 2003; Chwieroth 2007; Chinn and Ito 2008; Mosley and Singer 2008; Quinn and Toyoda 2008; Mukherjee and Singer 2010.

[49] King and Levine 1993; Levine 1997; Claessens et al. 2001; Rajan and Zingales 2003.

[50] Dobson and Jacquet 1998; Mattoo 1999; Tamirisa et al. 2000.

[51] Beck 2002; Chinn and Ito 2006; Aizenman and Noy 2009.

[52] For the determinants of free trade agreement proliferation, see Mansfield and Reinhardt 2003.

[53] World Bank WTI Database: Trade in Services (%) of GDP.

[54] World Bank. Employment in services (% of total employment) (modeled ILO estimate). 2019 Data.

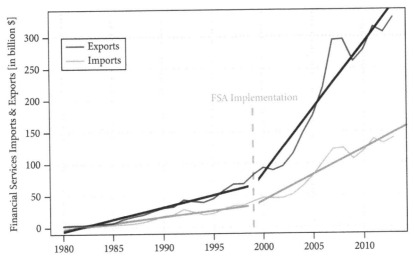

Figure 1.3 Financial services exports and imports, 1980–2013. Trade in financial services increased significantly after the implementation of the Financial Services Agreement. Data comes from UNCTAD. The most recent available data is from 2013. Period-specific regression lines are superimposed.

1.3 Research Design

This book analyzes quantitative and qualitative data to explore the puzzle of financial globalization. To understand the preferences and strategies of firms and governments, I interviewed trade negotiators, industry representatives, regulators, and international organization officials in Washington, DC; Brussels; Geneva; and Tokyo.[55] I also conducted archival research on US congressional testimony from industry representatives and trade negotiators, as well as international negotiation records and documents in the WTO digital archive. Further evidence comes from a variety of secondary sources, such as industry reports, firms' filings to the US Securities and Exchange Commission, and news articles on firms' investments, business relations, and international activities. The book also contains case

---

[55] These interviews served as background interviews for archival research and helped find written documents, such as reports, meeting transcripts, and correspondences (Mosley, 2013). Interviews with trade negotiators and industry officials were central to identifying the independent variable of industry linkage and the mechanism of industry coalitions.

14 MAKING FINANCIAL GLOBALIZATION

studies of international negotiations in financial services liberalization and financial regulatory developments in the US and China.

I utilize quantitative data to examine (1) what generates the cross-country variation in liberalization commitments and how this variation affects cross-border capital flows, (2) whether countries comply with the multilateral agreement and reform their domestic regulations, and (3) whether joining the multilateral agreement increases cross-border capital flows. To explore these questions, I introduce two new databases—one on financial trade restrictions in 102 countries and one on domestic financial regulations in 148 countries.[56]

The database on financial trade restrictions covers restrictions in countries' FSA liberalization commitments. It covers entry restrictions in 102 countries in all subsectors of financial services, including banking, insurance, securities, and auxiliary financial services. It delves deeply into specific restrictions in all modes of supply (modes 1–4) on ownership, equity, and personnel. For example, it includes restrictions on the percentage of foreign equity allowed for mergers and acquisitions, types of monopolies to be protected, and citizenship requirements for boards of directors.

The database on financial entry regulations covers domestic financial regulations regarding foreign entry in the financial sector in 148 countries from 1998 to 2007 (between the FSA negotiations and the global financial crisis). I gathered countries' foreign entry regulations to examine whether they have fulfilled their FSA commitments. The database includes financial entry regulations in banking, insurance, and securities, as well as regulations that create or strengthen independent regulators. It improves upon existing databases, such as the World Bank Regulation and Supervision Database,[57] by providing detailed information on regulations on foreign entry and independent regulation.

---

[56] These databases build on existing databases on trade in services (Francois et al. 2009; Dür et al. 2014; Martin 2011). Dür et al.'s database indicates whether a preferential trade agreement (PTA) contains a service chapter. Another database (Martin, 2011) covers service restrictions in PTAs for 53 countries and their 67 PTAs, which compares changes between a country's GATS commitments and subsequent PTA commitments in modes 1 and 3. Abiad et al. (2010) provide a database of financial reforms that examines entry barriers, but only in the banking sector.

[57] Barth et al. 2001.

1.4 Plan of the Book

This book develops a theory to explain why countries lowered their entry barriers in the financial industry and examines whether an international agreement led to changes in domestic regulatory reforms and economic flows around the world, leading to financial globalization. In Chapter 2, I analyze the preferences of firms and governments in financial services, present my theoretical framework of multilateral lobbying, and review alternative explanations. The theory of financial globalization shows how firms pushed for the creation of an international regime, which is often considered as state's domain. It demonstrates that understanding the preferences of firms and governments helps explain the push and pull of liberalization: who wants to liberalize, what they want to liberalize, and how (and why) countries vary in their level of liberalization.

In Chapter 3, I examine how firms are connected to the financial sector and how these financial linkages affect governments' preferences in financial globalization. I analyze firm- and industry-level data, and test the argument of financial linkages on countries' probability of joining the multilateral financial liberalization agreement. I find that countries with higher intersectoral financial linkages were more likely to join the international agreement. In Chapter 4, I explain the puzzle of fragmented liberalization in financial services—why governments liberalize financial services but include restrictions. I argue that countries with high levels of state ownership in the financial industry include more restrictions while liberalizing to control the pace and depth of foreign entry. I find that governments liberalize financial services to facilitate growth in the economy, but they include restrictions to control foreign operations in their markets as much as possible.

I then examine the de jure and de facto liberalization resulting from the multilateral agreement: whether it led to regulatory changes and economic flows around the world. In Chapter 5, I analyze countries' domestic financial regulatory reforms implemented as a result of their multilateral liberalization commitments. The FSA serves as a repository of domestic regulations around the world. Each country's liberalization schedule lists its past regulations, current regulatory changes, and future regulatory promises. I measure how many countries reformed their financial regulations based on these commitments. I also employ case studies to examine how firms used the FSA to change domestic financial regulations in the US and China, the

16 MAKING FINANCIAL GLOBALIZATION

two most sought-after financial markets. The agreement affected the US and Chinese regulatory developments in finance over the next 20 years.

In Chapter 6, I also study the FSA's effects on cross-border capital flows— trade in financial services, portfolio investment, and total FDI inflows.[58] While the literature on the effects of international economic agreements on economic outcomes has identified mixed effects,[59] I find that countries that joined the FSA experienced an increase in cross-border capital inflows. Chapter 7 concludes by discussing the implications of the study's findings for other international economic agreements.

---

[58] For studies on portfolio investment, see Mosley and Singer 2008. For studies on FDI, see N. M. Jensen 2008; Malesky 2009; Wellhausen 2014; Pandya 2014, among others.

[59] See Rose 2004; Goldstein et al. 2007; Tomz et al. 2007 for the GATT/WTO; Büthe and Milner 2008 for PTAs; and Jensen 2004 for the IMF.

2

A Theory of Financial Globalization

A core challenge in business and politics is the tug of war between firms and governments for control.[1] Firms want the autonomy to make their corporate governance decisions that best serve their interests, while governments have economic and political objectives, such as economic growth and political survival. This conflict is even more pronounced in relations between multinational corporations (MNCs) and host governments. Financial globalization is one of the most tense battlefields between multinational financial corporations (MFCs) and governments.

Finance is a politically and economically important sector for governments, which seek to strike a balance between maintaining control and generating economic growth. It is thus puzzling why 102 countries, including those without comparative advantages in financial services, committed to liberalize their financial markets by joining the 1997 World Trade Organization (WTO) Financial Services Agreement (FSA), and subsequently lowered domestic regulatory barriers to MFCs' entry.

A vast literature on financial liberalization has examined individual countries' decisions to liberalize their financial markets, including international and domestic explanations. International explanations include power asymmetry,[2] financial crises,[3] or diffusion across countries.[4] Domestic factors include regime type or characteristics of democracies—such as liberal values or median voters' preferences,[5] as well as the influence of interest groups that desire liberalization (or protection)—for countries' decisions about whether to open their financial markets.[6]

---

[1] Vernon 1971.
[2] Przeworski and Vreeland 2000; Drezner 2001; Mukherjee and Singer 2010.
[3] Haggard and Maxfield 1996; Mosley 2003; Abiad and Mody 2005; Martinez-Diaz 2009; Pepinsky 2012.
[4] Simmons and Elkins 2004; Quinn and Toyoda 2007.
[5] Quinn 2000; Milner and Mukherjee 2009; Jensen et al. 2012; Menaldo and Yoo 2015; Steinberg et al. 2018.
[6] Frieden 1991b; Brooks 2003; Chwieroth 2007; Danzman 2019.

Making Financial Globalization: How Firms Shape International Regulatory Cooperation. Clara Park,
Oxford University Press. © Oxford University Press 2025. DOI: 10.1093/oso/9780197761816.003.0002

18 MAKING FINANCIAL GLOBALIZATION

This book argues that firms pushed for the creation of an international liberalization agreement, which would reduce transaction costs of bilateral negotiations and establish international norms of liberalization. While the international relations literature mostly takes a state-centric view of regime creation, this study examines firms' multilateral lobbying efforts to establish an international agreement. It takes a comprehensive approach in examining firms' global lobbying campaigns, which include multilateral, bilateral, and domestic lobbying, to create a new international regime. It explores how firms formed coalitions across industries and countries to push for the creation of a new international regime in trade in financial services and enact contemporaneous changes in domestic regulations around the world.

By studying financial globalization through the lens of firms, this study investigates fundamental questions in international political economy: (1) why international economic agreements are created, who the main actors are, and where their preferences come from; (2) why the degree of liberalization varies across countries; and (3) what the effects of international economic agreements are. It examines the preferences of firms and governments in financial globalization and the mechanism through which firms created an international agreement that changed domestic regulations around the world.

The remainder of the chapter traces the source of preferences of the main actors of financial globalization—firms and governments—and how those preferences affect their strategies in financial globalization.[7] It then investigates the mechanism—industry coalitions—that translates firm preferences into international liberalization policies. It also discusses potential alternative explanations for financial globalization and how they relate to the framework developed in this book.

2.1 Preferences in Financial Globalization

What shapes the preferences of firms and governments in financial globalization? Traditional political economy models examine interest groups that lobby domestic politicians for protection or liberalization.[8] While these models do a good job of explaining the demand for domestic policies,

---

[7] Hoekman et al. 2007; Kose et al. 2009; Abraham and Schmukler 2018.
[8] Schattschneider 1935; Grossman and Helpman 1994; Gawande et al. 2012; Osgood 2021.

A THEORY OF FINANCIAL GLOBALIZATION   19

financial globalization involves stakeholders in multiple countries at different political, economic, and financial levels of development. These stakeholders include not only home and host governments but also MFCs, domestic producers of financial services (domestic financial firms), and users of financial services (MNCs and domestic firms that depend on financial services for inputs). Thus, understanding financial globalization requires a new framework that encompasses interests beyond the domestic financial industry.

I propose that two factors—financial linkage and government control over the financial industry—explain the demand for (and supply of) financial globalization. Financial linkage represents the financial industry's input-output linkage to other industries—how they use financial inputs such as loans, insurance, and securities in their production. Just as goods are intermediate inputs (e.g., steel is an intermediate input for automobiles), industrial firms also use (financial) services as inputs to produce their outputs.[9] For example, the automobile industry requires bank loans to buy machinery, insurance services for goods in transit (and employee pensions), and securities services for raising capital. Thus, financial linkages indicate the financial industry's centrality within the economy vis-à-vis other industries and the extent of financial dependence in the economy, which affects the preferences of MFCs and governments. Moreover, contrary to expectation, financial linkages differ from traditional economic measures, such as GDP or the level of financial development (see Chapter 3).[10]

Government control in the financial market refers to a government's direct ownership of state-owned financial institutions (SOFIs) or indirect shares in private financial firms. In contrast to the conventional wisdom of a *laissez-faire* approach to the financial market, many governments outside the US (and the UK) have directly or indirectly controlled their financial markets for economic and strategic reasons. These countries include developing countries as well as developed countries such as Austria, France, Germany, and Japan, where governments have traditionally exercised a high level of control over private firms in addition to SOFIs.[11] Government control of the financial market can proxy domestic financial service providers' opposition

---

[9] Indeed, previous studies have identified the manufacturing sector's demand for services inputs as the driving force behind the growth in services (Francois, 1990; Rowthorn and Ramaswamy, 1999). Service inputs account for a large part of the value added of manufacturing exports (Lodefalk 2014; Miroudot and Cadestin 2017; Hoekman and Shepherd 2017), especially in developing countries (Díaz-Mora et al., 2018).

[10] Cetorelli and Strahan 2006; Diebold and Yılmaz 2015.   [11] La Porta et al. 1999.

20 MAKING FINANCIAL GLOBALIZATION

to foreign entry in the financial market, since it is difficult to accurately measure the size of domestic opposition across countries. Government control of the financial market through SOFIs, which are public producers of financial services, can provide a lower bound measure of domestic financial firms' opposition.

Governments balance the dual objectives in financial services liberalization: political survival and economic growth. In the next section, I show how financial linkages and government control in the financial market affect the preferences of governments and MFCs in financial globalization.

2.1.1 Preferences of Governments in Financial Globalization

The source of governments' preferences in financial globalization has been a black box. Governments weigh the benefits and costs of financial liberalization. An important benefit is helping industrial firms access global financial services and capital. Foreign intermediate inputs can complement domestic inputs, and MFCs can help with cross-border export financing and bring in much-needed foreign direct investment (FDI).[12] Thus, financial liberalization can help domestic firms that depend on financial services as their inputs, such as those in agriculture, tourism, and light manufacturing.

However, financial market liberalization can be costly to governments, since many governments directly or indirectly control the financial sector for political and economic reasons. There are three main hypotheses for why governments control the financial industry. First, the *national security* hypothesis, which is rooted in the mercantilist idea, holds that governments control the flow of capital into and out of their countries to reduce dependence on foreign economic power.[13] Second, the *developmental* hypothesis holds that governments channel investments to economically weak but politically important groups that private banks may not serve.[14] For example, private enterprises may not serve high-cost/low-revenue groups such as

---

[12] Danzman (2019) examines how domestic firms lobby for FDI liberalization to attract more foreign capital.

[13] For a discussion of opposition to inward FDI in China, see Tingley et al. 2015.

[14] Pigou 1924; Gerschenkron 1962; Haggard 1990; Amsden 1992; Rodrik 1995; Haggard and Maxfield 1996; Megginson and Netter 2001.

A THEORY OF FINANCIAL GLOBALIZATION   21

infant industries, the rural population, or public projects (e.g., infrastructure), but governments have political incentives to help these groups. Thus, governments control the financial industry to channel investments across groups. Third, the *rent-seeking* hypothesis states that governments seek to strategically apportion capital to their selectorates in order to maintain their hold on power.[15] Due to the fungibility of money in the public and private spheres, the finance sector tends to have close ties to government leaders and their families.[16] Thus, many governments exert either direct control through SOFIs or indirect control by regulating private financial firms.

Yet government ownership of financial firms does not come cheap: costs increase over time for two main reasons. First, state ownership of financial firms places a heavy burden on a country's fiscal budget because nonperforming loans to state-owned enterprises (SOEs) increase the government debt. For example, the rise of nonperforming loans has led to economic crises, such as the Asian financial crisis in the 1990s and Japan's asset bubble in the 1990s.[17] Second, many SOFIs suffer from technological backwardness and soft budget constraint problems.[18] Since the government provides them with capital when needed, many SOFIs have few incentives to innovate and tend to be less productive (and profitable) than their private counterparts.[19] Since MFCs are more technologically developed, their entry can help domestic user firms save money and time in their cross-border financial transactions.

For these reasons, I expect government preferences to vary based on the level of financial linkage and its (desired) level of direct control in the financial market. Because the financial industry is strategically important for governments, they carefully weigh the diffuse benefits for the economy (financial linkage) against the concentrated costs of liberalization (losing state control). I expect financial linkage to provide the push for liberalization and

---

[15] Krueger 1974; Shleifer and Vishny 1994; Dinç 2005; Faccio 2006; Micco et al. 2007.

[16] Claessens 2006; Claessens and Perotti 2007; Caprio et al. 2010.

[17] See Shleifer and Vishny 1997; Lu et al. 2005; Cornett et al. 2010; Zhang et al. 2016; Baudino and Yun 2017.

[18] La Porta and Lopez-de Silanes 1999; Roland 2000; Shleifer and Vishny 2002; Kornai et al. 2003; Weill 2003.

[19] The inefficiencies of state-owned enterprises led to a call for privatization in Eastern Europe in the 1990s and China in the 2000s (Lin et al. 1998), although some argue that privatization yields fewer benefits than is generally assumed. See Roland 2000; Megginson and Netter 2001; Bartel and Harrison 2005. See Malesky and Taussig 2009 for Vietnam.

22 MAKING FINANCIAL GLOBALIZATION

Table 2.1 Predicted Liberalization as Function of Financial Linkage and Government Control in the Financial Industry

	Low Government Control	High Government Control
Low Financial Linkage	Status quo	Protection
High Financial Linkage	Full liberalization	Fragmented liberalization

the level of government control to pull away from liberalization. Table 2.1 presents a typology of financial services liberalization. The degree of liberalization can be ranked in terms of openness from full liberalization to fragmented liberalization, status quo, and protection.

When financial linkage is low but government control is high (top right cell), a government is likely to protect its financial industry, which is dominated by SOFIs. The benefits of liberalization are low due to low financial linkage in the economy and the costs are high because of the high level of government control; therefore, governments are unlikely to liberalize their financial sector. However, when financial linkage is high but government control is low (bottom left), governments are expected to open up their financial sector because the benefits outweigh the costs.

When the level of financial linkage and government control are both low (top left), a country is predicted to maintain the status quo, since government has no particular reasons to liberalize further than the current level. When financial linkage and government control are both high (bottom right), fragmented liberalization is likely: governments liberalize their financial markets due to the spillover effects from high financial linkages, but they include restrictions to control the pace of liberalization.

Figure 2.1 depicts this relationship: countries with more financial linkages and greater government control over the financial market are likely to have more restrictions than those with less government bank control. When government control is low, financial linkages have few effects on the degree of conditionality (restrictions). However, as government control in the financial sector increases, linkages have a greater effect on restrictions. Since financial linkages are high, governments liberalize to help industrial firms access the global financial network, but as government control over the financial market is also high, they embed restrictions in areas of strategic importance in order to control the speed of liberalization. I further explore government preferences in financial services liberalization in Chapter 4.

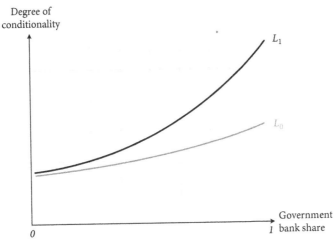

Figure 2.1 Government control moderates the effect of financial linkage on the number of conditions imposed in liberalization schedules. This figure illustrates the effect of moving from low (L_0) to high (L_1) levels of financial linkage on the number of restrictions as a function of government control of banks.

2.1.2 Preferences of Multinational Financial Corporations

Financial linkage explains why MFCs demand an international framework. Firms seek to maximize profits by either increasing revenues or cutting costs. To increase revenues, they try to sell more to existing clients and also find new clients (e.g., the IT company Apple could either try to sell more products to existing users or look for new customers). Similarly, for financial services, international business opportunities shape their preferences in financial globalization: following their existing clients to new markets and finding new clients around the world.

Financial firms expand overseas to follow their corporate clients' international expansion in what is known as the "follow-the-client" hypothesis in the international business literature (similar to the "follow-the-flag" hypothesis in international relations).[20] When MFCs' clients—e.g., MNCs in the agricultural, manufacturing, and services industries—expand overseas in search of cheaper inputs and new markets, they need to transfer capital

---

[20] Previous studies have used this hypothesis to understand firms' internationalization strategies. See Dunning 1980; Yannopoulos 1983; Boddewyn et al. 1986; Pollins 1989; Gowa 1995; Mansfield 1995; Biglaiser and DeRouen 2007; Manova 2013.

24 MAKING FINANCIAL GLOBALIZATION

across borders, insure their goods in transit, and advise on mergers and acquisitions of local firms and factories.[21]

However, in their pursuit of international expansion, MFCs often faced three main types of entry barriers in the host country's regulatory environment. The first problem MFCs encountered was the lack of *market access*, in which several governments limited or blocked MFCs' entry into their markets. For example, many of them limited the type of financial businesses allowed in their markets by foreign financial firms, such as by introducing geographic and ownership restrictions. Second, MFCs faced a lack of *transparency* in host countries' regulations, as many governments applied them on a case-by-case basis; MFCs hired brokers to navigate regulatory processes. The third issue was *discrimination*: some governments had tighter restrictions for foreign firms than for domestic firms, such as higher capital requirements for opening a financial firm, which boosted the entry costs for MFCs.

As MFCs attempted to enter more markets, so did the transaction costs of bilateral negotiations over these entry barriers. Thus, they decided to advocate the creation of a central international forum to reduce transaction costs through an agreed set of norms, principles, rules, and procedures.[22] MFCs wanted an international framework that would create norms on market access, transparency, and nondiscrimination in many countries at once. They also sought an independent regulator in host markets to ensure fair competition. I therefore expect financial linkage to explain the demand for financial globalization: which countries MFCs try to enter, what financial services they seek to provide in the new markets, and the desired level of liberalization in countries of interest when following their MNC clients abroad.[23]

2.2 A Theory of Financial Globalization

I develop my theory of financial globalization in four main stages, as depicted in Figure 2.2. First, when multinational financial firms expand abroad to provide their corporate clients with cross-border financial

---

[21] MFCs also help organize international initial public offerings of firms as well as governments in host markets by issuing bonds in the international market.
[22] Ruggie 1982; Krasner 1982; Aggarwal 1998.   [23] Grandori and Soda 1995; Kinne 2013.

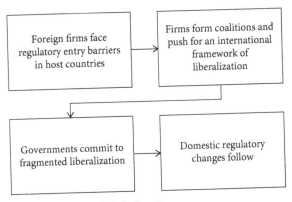

Figure 2.2 Process of financial globalization.

services, they face entry barriers in host countries, especially those with a high degree of state ownership in the financial industry. The bilateral bargaining costs of negotiating entry increase as MFCs enter more countries. In order to consolidate all bilateral negotiations and reduce their transaction costs, firms seek to create an international framework. To effectively pressure home and host governments, firms create two types of industry coalitions—international intra-industry and domestic inter-industry coalitions—and develop the norms, principles, rules, and procedures for a new international regime.[24] These coalitions work with home governments as well as host governments and international organizations to increase support for the international agreement.

Governments, in turn, agree to liberalize their financial markets to attract foreign capital and services for the domestic industries, especially for those industries in which they have comparative advantages. However, in an effort to protect domestic financial firms, some of which are state-owned, governments include restrictions in their multilateral liberalization commitments to protect their control over the politically important market (i.e., retail banking) while liberalizing financial services that would benefit their industrial firms (i.e., commercial banking). After joining a multilateral liberalization agreement, governments gradually implement domestic regulatory reforms, depending on the institutional arrangements at home.

---

[24] Haas 1980; Ruggie 1982; Krasner 1983; Aggarwal 1985.

26 MAKING FINANCIAL GLOBALIZATION

1. Foreign financial firms face entry barriers in host countries. Governments erect barriers to entry in financial markets due to the strategic importance of the financial industry.[25] Foreign services providers face three main types of entry barriers in host markets: bilateral bargaining costs, entrenched domestic interests, and the lack of an independent regulator in host countries.

First, foreign firms face costly bilateral bargaining with host governments, each of which has idiosyncratic entry requirements. Uncertainty about if, when, and how to enter host countries makes it difficult for firms to plan for their future operations. Thus, firms must conduct extensive market research on local laws and customs in each host country before applying for an entry license, and then try to build networks with powerful local politicians and business leaders. These search costs multiply as the number of desired destinations increases.

Even if foreign firms are given permission to enter, they face a second obstacle: their main competitor is often an established domestic firm with close ties to the government, or a SOFI that enjoys unfair advantages over foreign firms. SOFIs have explicit state backing as they help governments achieve their political goals. Therefore, they receive preferential treatment from the government and are less cost-constrained than their private counterparts.[26] This presents challenges to MFCs that lack these preferential treatments from host governments.

The third type of entry barrier for foreign firms is the lack of an independent regulator in many countries. This is a significant problem because the government ministry responsible for approving foreign entry and monitoring fair competition is often the same entity that operates the SOFI. This creates a conflict of interest for regulators in terms of fair market competition.

Therefore, foreign firms face insurmountable problems in foreign entry. Each entrant firm lacks bargaining leverage and cannot force every host country to create an independent regulator. Nor can firms force host countries to privatize SOFIs and ensure competition. A solution to these problems is an international framework that can change state behavior and enact contemporaneous changes in many countries. This type of framework can create international norms and principles for independent regulation and

---

[25] Stigler (1971) referred to producers demanding regulation to deter entry for their own protection. In this case, the government is the dominant producer in the industry.
[26] Kornai 1980; Maskin 1996; Roland 2000.

competition, decrease the transaction costs of bilateral bargaining, and reduce uncertainty and information asymmetry.[27]

2. Firms form coalitions to push for an international liberalization framework. While firms cannot directly participate in international negotiations, they can push governments to create and facilitate such talks by providing pressure, information, and incentives to government negotiators. Firms play two main supporting roles in international negotiations, by (1) providing the language of the regime (norms, principles, rules, and procedures) to home and host governments as well as international organizations and (2) educating and offering incentives to host governments. I discuss each role here in turn.

In the first role, firms influence the creation of a new regime by providing the language of the new regime and the desired outcome of the negotiations. Particularly in technologically advanced sectors, such as finance, governments rely on firms to provide information on their international competition since they are at the forefront of commercial expansion.[28] Firms inform their home governments about the types of behind-the-border regulatory barriers they face in particular countries, and about which types of businesses they wish to be protected at home and liberalized abroad.[29] Furthermore, firms advocate norms—such as independent regulation, transparent regulatory processes, and nondiscrimination—in the international framework.

Second, firms also facilitate trade negotiations by educating and offering incentives to host governments. Governments in developing countries are more likely to be persuaded of the benefits of liberalization when multinational firms visit the country and promise investment. Industry representatives help convince host governments, even in countries that do not have large financial markets, that liberalizing financial services can have positive potential spillover effects in the economy and help boost the country's economic productivity by bringing in external capital, technology, and management practices in the financial industry.

---

[27] Abbott and Snidal 1998.   [28] Woll and Artigas 2007.   [29] Milner and Yoffie 1989.

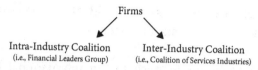

Figure 2.3 Industry coalitions designed to increase firms' bargaining leverage.

Since no single firm has sufficient resources or power to create an international framework on its own, firms form industry coalitions within and across borders to influence international policymaking and trade negotiations.[30] Financial linkages provide insights into industry coalition formation. If financial firms had focused only within the financial industry, they may not have garnered much support for an international liberalization agreement, especially from countries that do not have comparative advantages in finance. However, linkages to other industries helped unite several industries that use financial services from multiple firms, industries, and countries and made the liberalization agreement more appealing to a broader set of interest groups, which can push multiple governments concurrently. Financial linkages generate network effects: the more countries that sign the multilateral agreement, the greater the benefits of financial globalization.[31]

Firms create two types of coalitions—international intra-industry coalitions and domestic inter-industry coalitions—to obtain the necessary resources to mount an international lobbying campaign as well as the political leverage to pressure politicians at home and abroad, as shown in Figure 2.3. First, international intra-industry coalitions are composed of business leaders in the same industry from different countries. Firms create such associations to pressure multiple governments simultaneously and to create a consensus among firms in order to shape the outcome according to their preferences. Firms hold meetings that facilitate the exchange of ideas and concerns as well as agreement on best practices; they pass this information, along with relevant technical details, to government negotiators. Industry coalitions also publicize the benefits of liberalization through policy reports and media campaigns.[32]

---

[30] Narlikar 2003.
[31] Network effects also apply to other service industries that serve as a platform for other sectors, such as IT and telecommunications (e.g., Amazon and Facebook).
[32] Freeman 2000.

The most significant benefit of an international industry consensus is that it can help break domestic gridlock. As Putnam (1988) showed, government negotiators often spend as much, if not more, time negotiating with domestic interest groups as with each other. If domestic interest groups across borders reach a consensus and present uniform demands to their respective governments, government officials can no longer argue that their firms are against opening up. This reduces the number of domestic negotiations and facilitates international negotiations.

Second, domestic inter-industry associations include domestic industries that use financial services for inputs (financial linkage). These cross-cutting coalitions increase electoral leverage on domestic politicians to advocate and support trade liberalization in a given sector. A single industry may be unable to persuade the national legislature or the executive branch to push for a trade agreement in its sector. However, as more industries (and congressional districts) align their interests, they can pressure more members of Congress to advance their trade agenda. The history of trade in financial services negotiations demonstrates how a network of industry representatives and government officials works together to create an international framework of trade in services.[33]

3. Governments commit to liberalization but include restrictions. Governments joined the FSA and liberalized their financial markets, despite the costs to their domestic financial firms, to attract external capital and global financial services to their domestic industries, such as manufacturing and tourism, in which they have comparative advantages.[34] As the world financial market becomes more integrated, exporters and importers benefit from seamless cross-border financial transactions, while domestic firms gain more foreign investment. By allowing MFCs to enter their markets, governments can help their domestic firms, such as in the mining and manufacturing industries in which they have comparative advantages, access external capital and financial services.[35] Moreover, the need for financial market liberalization increases as the technological gap widens between foreign and domestic financial firms.[36] Opening up the financial sector

---

[33] For studies on networks in international relations, see Aggarwal and Koo 2005; Jung and Lake 2011; Oatley et al. 2013; Kinne 2013; Reisenbichler 2015; Dorussen et al. 2016; MacDonald 2018.
[34] Aitken and Harrison 1999; Javorcik 2004; Bekaert et al. 2011; Danzman 2019.
[35] Markusen 1989; Frieden 1991b; Deardorff 2001.   [36] Andrews 1994.

30 MAKING FINANCIAL GLOBALIZATION

attracts foreign firms with advanced technology and helps industrial firms that depend on financial inputs to access a variety of financial services.[37]

The paradox of fragmented liberalization, though, occurs when governments must balance the interests of nonfinancial firms (for more capital) and domestic financial firms (for protection).[38] Liberalization introduces competition to domestic financial firms and SOFIs. However, even if governments are persuaded by the positive spillover effects, including foreign capital and technology, they may initially be hesitant to open up multilaterally.

Since liberalization can erode domestic firms' market share, governments include restrictions in an attempt to maximize the benefits of liberalization while minimizing the costs to domestic firms. More restrictions are expected for countries with a high share of government ownership in the financial industry, as they would directly face the consequences of foreign competition. Moreover, countries cannot easily renege on their multilateral liberalization commitments, since they are legally bound by the WTO's enforcement (dispute settlement) mechanism, which can hold them accountable if they fail to live up to their commitments.

Thus, governments embedded restrictions in their multilateral liberalization commitments, such as geographic restrictions (China) and the state-by-state insurance restriction (US), to protect their domestic financial firms during liberalization. The increasing importance of finance for economic growth pushes governments to liberalize their long-closed financial markets—but to also include more restrictions while liberalizing to protect their control in the financial market.

4. Countries implement domestic regulatory reforms. An international agreement pushes governments to reform their domestic regulations to follow through on their multilateral commitments. As governments commit to lowering behind-the-border regulatory entry barriers, they undertake domestic regulatory reforms in keeping with their international liberalization commitments, such as nondiscrimination for MFCs and independent financial regulators. However, the timeline for implementing these regulatory changes varies across countries, depending on domestic politics, elections, and legislative processes.

---

[37] Markusen 1989; Frieden 1991b; Deardorff 2001; Rajan and Zingales 2003; Brooks 2004.

[38] Domestic incumbent firms' fear of competing with foreign entrants, often large and more efficient multinational firms, has been well established in the literature. See Claessens et al. 2001; Rajan and Zingales 2003; Micco et al. 2007; Pepinsky 2013.

2.3 Mechanism for Multilateral Lobbying

U.S. negotiators consulted frequently with U.S. financial services representatives to gain their insight. These institutions were extremely active during the [FSA] negotiations in engaging foreign governments and foreign financial services companies and identifying areas of common interest.

—US Department of the Treasury, 1998[39]

How do firms translate their preferences for financial services liberalization into international policies? I argue that the key mechanism is the industry coalitions they built across industries and countries. Using a process-tracing approach, I demonstrate that firms shaped the international governing framework in trade in financial services by forming cross-sector and cross-country industry coalitions. These coalitions increased the number of stakeholders and provided the language of the new international regime to government negotiators by working with home and host governments as well as an international organization.

Starting in the late 1970s, financial firms increased their international expansion as technological developments facilitated cross-border financial transactions. However, they soon faced barriers to entry in host countries. Governments in many markets were hesitant to fully open their markets to MFCs due to fears of losing control of their financial markets. In response, they erected entry barriers, such as nontransparent entry processes and idiosyncratic domestic regulations. Three MFCs that especially lamented these entry barriers were American Express, AIG, and Citi.

Entry barriers hit the bottom line of American Express, which needed to facilitate real-time transactions with hotels, restaurants, and airlines for its credit cards to be effective. In addition to its credit card business, American Express also had a large commercial banking division, Shearson Lehman (which was later spun off as Lehman Brothers), which sought to expand overseas in order to facilitate M&As and securities services. However, market access problems stymied seamless cross-border transactions.

Similarly, AIG, an insurer that has operated internationally, was also facing market access problems—particularly in Asia. AIG especially wanted to expand its business in Japan, which had the second-largest economy in the

---

[39] US Department of the Treasury 1998, p. 116.

32 MAKING FINANCIAL GLOBALIZATION

world at the time and high rates of savings, but it faced barriers to entering the country's insurance market. In Japan, foreign firms such as AIG could only operate in the tertiary sector (accident and health insurance), not in the profitable primary (life) and secondary (general, auto, property, and casualty) insurance sectors, which domestic firms dominated.[40] AIG also faced market access problems in other countries in Asia, such as Malaysia and India. Citi also faced barriers to entering many global markets during its international expansion.

The leaders of AIG, American Express, and Citi learned that each was facing similar problems internationally when they served on the President's Trade Advisory Committee together. Then-AIG CEO Maurice Greenberg had served on the President's Advisory Board for Trade Negotiations for over 30 years. James D. Robinson III, then-CEO of American Express, was widely known as the Commercial Secretary of State because of his deep involvement in international trade and finance policies. John S. Reed, then-CEO of Citi, chaired a Services Policy Advisory Committee to the US Trade Representative (USTR).[41] While their businesses differed, they faced common problems such as bilateral entry negotiations, which increased their transaction costs and uncertainty. They wanted to promote liberalization norms around the world in order to reduce these transaction costs.

Serving on government advisory boards gave these leaders the idea of developing an international agreement that could enact contemporaneous regulatory changes around the world and open up global financial markets to their entry. Such an agreement would create norms, principles, rules, and procedures for liberalization that apply to all countries. Yet since creating a multilateral framework requires considerable time and resources, they recruited other firms to pool resources and increase their leverage.

Firms formed international, intra-industry, and domestic intersectoral coalitions to persuade their home governments, host governments, and international institutions to create a regime. Within the US, financial firms formed an inter-industry association—the Coalition of Services Industries (CSI)—in 1982 with other service providers, such as finance, telecommunications, professional, travel, tourism, transportation, and information

---

[40] Greenberg and Cunningham 2013.

[41] Steve Forbes, "Hank Greenberg on Turning AIG into a Global Giant," *Forbes*, March 25, 2013; Greenberg and Cunningham 2013; Kelsey 2008; Aronson and Feketekuty 1991; Gerhard Peters and John T. Woolley, "Ronald Reagan: Appointment of 16 Members of the Advisory Committee for Trade Negotiations," The American Presidency Project: https://tinyurl.com/2mkawt72.

A THEORY OF FINANCIAL GLOBALIZATION   33

technology services, to broaden the push for services liberalization domestically and internationally.[42] They also helped firms in 23 other countries create their own CSIs, including in the EU, Hong Kong, and Singapore.[43]

In addition to the multisector coalition in the US, a multicountry intra-industry coalition emerged in the financial industry. The FSA negotiations were the "first negotiations in which a multinational industry group," such as financial firms and associations from different countries, organized to "advocate liberalization of services trade."[44] Financial companies and associations from the US, Canada, UK, EU, Hong Kong, Japan, and Australia formed the Financial Leaders Group (FLG) in 1996. Figure 2.4 shows members of the FLG, which includes executives from American Express, AIG, Bank of America, Barclays, Chase, and Morgan Stanley, as well as insurers from France (GAN), Italy (Assicurazioni Generali), and Hong Kong (Trade Development Council). They came together to "provide private support for government efforts to reduce barriers."[45] The FLG compiled an "agreed lists of barriers" in banking, securities, insurance, and other financial services, as well as requests to remove specific barriers in "20 key markets in Asia, Latin America, Africa, and Eastern Europe."[46] At the 1996 World Economic Forum in Davos, the FLG issued a statement of "Objectives of Financial Services Negotiations," which it referred to as a "bill of rights" for the global financial services trade.[47]

CEOs of international financial firms also formed the Financial Leaders Working Group (FLWG) to "present a common agenda to their governments' negotiators" (see Figure 2.5).[48] The members included the CEOs of the firms in the FLG as well as industry association leaders in the US (CSI, National Association of Insurance Brokers, and Securities Industry Association), Canada (Canadian Bankers Association), UK (British Invisibles), France (Fédération Française des Sociétés D'Assurances and

---

[42] Feketekuty 1988; Freeman 2000. The CSI's "overriding objective has been to obtain commercially significant trade liberalization in financial and payments services, express delivery and logistics, telecommunications, energy, computer-related, travel and tourism, audio-visual, accounting and legal services" (Vastine 2005, p. 4). Also see US House of Representatives 1999.

[43] The CSI continues to advocate services liberalization through the Uruguay Round, Doha Round, Trans-Pacific Partnership, Trans-Atlantic Trade and Investment Partnership, and Trade in Services Agreement negotiations.

[44] Vastine 2005, p. 2.

[45] Vastine Testimony, House Ways and Means Committee, February 26, 1997, p. 117.

[46] Vastine 2005, p. 2.

[47] This gathering has been described as "the catalyst for key international meetings among US and EC negotiators, and business representatives" (Vastine Testimony, p. 117).

[48] Vastine 2005, p. 2.

34 MAKING FINANCIAL GLOBALIZATION

FINANCIAL LEADERS GROUP

Co-Chairmen

Andrew Buxton
Chairman, Barclays Bank PLC

Ken Whipple
President, Ford Financial Services Group

Members

Jean Jacques Bonnaud
Former President, GAN

Victor Fung
Chairman, Hong Kong Trade Development Council

Bruce Galloway
Vice Chairman, Royal Bank of Canada

Richard K. Goeltz
Vice Chairman and Chief Financial Officer, American Express Company

Evan Greenberg
Executive Vice President, American International Group, Inc.

David Holbrook
Chairman, Marsh & McLennan Incorporated

Douglas Hurd
Deputy Chairman, NatWest Markets

David Komansky
President, Merrill Lynch & Co., Inc.

Mariano De Martino
Director, Assicurazioni Generali SpA

Rodney McLauchlan
Managing Director, Bankers Trust Securities Corporation

Peter Middleton
Chief Executive, Salomon Brothers International, Inc.

Dean R. O'Hare
Chairman and Chief Executive Officer, The Chubb Corporation

John Price
Managing Director, Government Affairs, The Chase Manhattan Bank

Robert Pozen
Managing Director and General Counsel, Fidelity Investments

Ralph Schauss
Group Executive, Bank of America

Sir David Walker
Executive Chairman, Morgan Stanley Group (Europe) PLC

Figure 2.4 Members of the Financial Leaders Group.
Source: WTO Singapore Ministerial Meeting Hearing (1997), p. 121.

Crédit Industriel et Commercial de Paris), and Europe (Comité Européen des Assurances and Fédération Bancaire de L'Union Européenne). The US domestic intra-industry coalitions within the financial industry, such as the Securities Industry Association and the American Council of Life Insurance, also wrote letters to the Senate and House Banking Committees for the FSA.[49]

---

[49] "Industry Letter on Financial Services Deal," *Inside US Trade*, December 15, 1997. Other intra-industry coalitions include the Investment Company Institute, the National Association of Insurance Brokers, the International Insurance Council, and the Bankers Association for Foreign Trade.

A THEORY OF FINANCIAL GLOBALIZATION 35

FINANCIAL LEADERS WORKING GROUP (FLWG)

Alastair Ballantyne
Vice President, Morgan Stanley Group (Europe) PLC

Sir Nicholas Bayne
Chairman, LOTIS Committee, British Invisibles

Josh Bolten
Executive Director, Goldman Sachs (London)

Nickolaus Bömcke
Secretary General, Federation Bancaire de L'Union Europeenne

Bill Canis
Vice President, International Corporate Affairs, American Express Company

Thomas Dawson
Director, Financial Institutions Group, Merrill Lynch & Co., Inc.

Brant Free
Vice President, International External Affairs, The Chubb Corporation

Harry Hassanwalia
Deputy Chief Economist, Royal Bank of Canada

Bill Hawley
Vice President and Director, International Government Relations
Citicorp/Citibank

Jean-Luc Herrenschmidt
Director, International Affairs, Credit Industriel et Commercial de Paris

Oakley Johnson
Senior Vice President, Corporate Affairs, American International Group

Steve Judge
Senior Vice President, Government Affairs, Securities Industry Association

Bob Kramer
Vice President, Policy Analysis and Development, Bank of America

Bruce Kulp
Executive Director, Strategic Planning and External Affairs
Ford Financial Services Group

Patrick Lefas
Director, International Affairs,
Fédération Française des Sociétés D'Assurances

Jacques Leglu
Deputy Secretary General, Comité Européen des Assurances

Carl Modecki
President, National Association of Insurance Brokers

Marlene Nicholson
Director, Government Relations, Barclays Bank PLC

Mary Podesta
Associate Counsel, International, Investment Company Institute

Raymond Protti
President and Chief Executive Officer, Canadian Bankers Association

Peter Russell
Vice President, Government Affairs, The Chase Manhattan Bank

John Standen
Chief Executive Officer, Emerging Markets, Barclays Bank PLC

Bob Vastine
President, Coalition of Service Industries

Figure 2.5 Members of the Financial Leaders Working Group.
Source: WTO Singapore Ministerial Meeting (1997), p. 122.

36 MAKING FINANCIAL GLOBALIZATION

These industry coalitions served four main functions: forum shopping, agenda setting, consensus building, and advocacy. First, they engaged in forum shopping, which has long been considered the domain of states,[50] to find a home for the international negotiations. Since the existing framework on tariffs, the General Agreement on Tariffs and Trade (GATT), did not apply to trade in services, multinational firms proceeded with a blank canvas: they sought to help create new rules instead of adapting the existing ones.[51] Thus, they picked the WTO, a trade organization, instead of international financial organizations, such as the International Monetary Fund (IMF) or the Bank for International Settlements, to create a new framework from scratch.

Second, industry coalitions helped set the agenda by advocating norms, such as transparency and independent regulation, which became an annex to the General Agreement on Trade in Services (GATS), called Understanding on Financial Services, that the FSA signatories adopted upon signing. Firms not only supplied a list of trade barriers but also the new norms, principles, rules, and procedures for a new regime. Government negotiators were often unfamiliar with the entry barriers that firms faced during commercial expansion.[52] Coalitions therefore worked with the USTR office to influence the language of the policies on trade in services.[53] Georgetown Law Professor Robert Stumberg testified in a Senate hearing, stating: "If you look at the US schedule of GATS commitments, which is the progeny of the Coalition of Service Industries work in partnership with USTR over more than a decade, you will see that there are a number of specific sector commitments that represent the priorities of the United States in terms of those big markets."[54]

Third, they helped build a consensus among firms. The common problem in international negotiations is that governments use domestic industry as an excuse for limited liberalization. However, in the FSA negotiations, firms in multiple countries converged on a set of demands facilitated by industry coalitions. As Putnam (1988) pointed out in his two-level analysis of international negotiations that Level II players (domestic interest groups)

---

[50] Busch 2007.   [51] Freeman 1998.

[52] Aronson and Feketekuty 1991; Greenberg 2003.

[53] The Omnibus Tariff and Trade Act of 1984 defined the US negotiating objectives for trade in services. The act "directs the USTR to develop and coordinate the implementation of US policies concerning trade in services. Requires federal agencies responsible for regulating any service sector industry to advise and work with the USTR concerning: (1) the treatment afforded US services sector's interest in foreign markets; or (2) allegations of unfair practices by foreign governments or companies in a service sector." H.R. 3398—Omnibus Tariff and Trade Act of 1984, 98th Congress (1983–1984).

[54] See Aggarwal 1992; Sherman 1998; Senate 2005.

A THEORY OF FINANCIAL GLOBALIZATION   37

across countries could contact each other directly, firms formed an industry consensus across borders to concurrently push hesitant governments.

Fourth, industry coalitions engaged in advocacy. They coined the term "trade in services" and worked tirelessly to promote it in newspapers and to politicians, media, and the public. If journalists did not use the term—trade in services—correctly in early days when the new vocabulary was still fresh, lobbyists would call newspapers to ensure they used the new term, "trade in services" (Freeman, 2000). To increase the number of interest groups lobbying governments for liberalization, coalitions broadened the scope of negotiations beyond financial services to liberalizing *all* trade in services.

Thus, industry coalitions engaged in a multifront battle to advocate the worldwide liberalization of trade in services. These coalitions directly lobbied politicians. The intra- and inter-industry private sector coalitions traveled together to persuade governments around the world and present a unified stance.[55] They met with government negotiators and discussed the benefits of liberalization and how their investments could benefit local economies.[56] They met with government negotiators from 20 countries that the "FLWG had targeted as of most interest."[57] The private sector also attended the GATT ministerial meetings in 1980, 1982, 1984, 1986, and the Uruguay Round.[58] Near the end of the negotiations, representatives of "as many as 40 companies and associations in Europe and North America regularly met jointly with the chief financial services negotiators of both the EU and the U.S."[59]

The negotiations to open financial markets around the world were intense. For example, US financial firms lobbied Senator Alfonse D'Amato from New York, who was chair of the Senate Banking Committee during the FSA negotiations, to push USTR and Treasury officials to gain more concessions from other countries.[60] Senator D'Amato, along with Senator Paul Sarbanes (D-MD), stressed to US negotiators—Treasury Secretary Robert Rubin and USTR Charlene Barshefsky—that a compromise would "seriously and unwisely handicap U.S. firms."[61]

---

[55] Interview with a financial industry lobbyist, Brussels, July 2017.

[56] Drake and Nicolaidis 1992.   [57] Vastine 2005, p. 2.

[58] Freeman 2000.   [59] Vastine 2005, p. 2.

[60] D'Amato, Sarbanes Letter on Financial Services to Robert Rubin and Charlene Barshefsky, December 3, 1997; House Letter on Financial Services to Robert Rubin and Charlene Barshefsky, December 5, 1997, in *Inside US Trade*, December 12, 1997; G. Jonquieres, "Happy End to a Cliff Hanger." *Financial Times*, December 15, 1997.

[61] AIG and its political action committee donated money to both main US parties: $485,440 to Republicans and $442,990 to Democrats. Senator D'Amato received $18,250 from AIG. Bhusan Bahree and Helene Cooper, "AIG, Malaysia's Mahathir Peril WTO Accord to Open Markets," *The Wall Street Journal*, December 10, 1997.

38 MAKING FINANCIAL GLOBALIZATION

Malaysia especially presented a serious problem for AIG, as the government only allowed a minority ownership through the FSA when AIG already had 100% ownership in its Malaysian entity, which meant it would have to divest 51% of its assets. On the last day of the negotiations (December 12), the US added a most-favored-nation carve-out for Malaysia for its insurance restrictions in the FSA. Then the US negotiators called AIG's CEO Hank Greenberg at 2 a.m., who finally agreed to the end of the FSA negotiations.[62] Industry coalitions picked the international forum, provided the norms and principles, set the negotiating agenda, and lobbied home and host governments and international organizations, and finally succeeded in creating an international framework that opened financial markets around the world.

2.4 Quiet Politics and Financial Globalization

Trade (in goods) negotiations have traditionally pitted labor and capital groups against each other and generated public opposition.[63] Yet there has been little public awareness of (financial) services liberalization and no labor opposition, for three main reasons: it often creates jobs, rather than displacing jobs, as in goods liberalization; the service industry has low asset specificity; and liberalization generates widespread benefits for consumers *and* producers.

First, trade in services liberalization often *creates* jobs, since the services are mostly provided near the consumer's location.[64] For example, a financial firm that opens a branch in a host country will not only bring its top leadership from the headquarters but also hire local bankers who can better serve local clients and navigate the domestic policy and social environment; it is also too expensive to bring in all foreign bankers. Therefore, labor owners in host markets can benefit from services trade liberalization through the increase in the demand for labor from foreign service providers.

Second, the asset specificity of the services sector is lower than that of the manufacturing sector. Domestic workers can relatively more easily change jobs in the services sector than in the manufacturing sector. For example,

---

[62] Greenberg and Cunningham 2013.
[63] Scheve and Slaughter 2001, 2004; Mayda and Rodrik 2005; O'Rourke and Sinnott 2006.
[64] Konan and Maskus 2006; J. B. Jensen 2008; Hijzen et al. 2011; Manning et al. 2012.

A THEORY OF FINANCIAL GLOBALIZATION   39

marketing professionals can move across industries and from domestic to foreign firms (and vice versa). Ironically, this flexibility prevents local service firms from building political coalitions against foreign entry because such firms are more mobile than manufacturing firms, which frequently hire thousands of people in a factory town, often for decades. People in factory towns depend on the company to provide livelihoods for generations; in return, the company builds lasting political connections in the area that oppose trade liberalization or offshoring. The services industry is much more mobile; many services jobs simply require storefronts or office buildings, and they can easily move to where the labor and clients are. Thus, in trade in financial services liberalization, there has not been a sharp division between labor and capital as there has been for trade in goods.[65]

The third reason that financial services liberalization has not produced a public outcry is that consumers *and* producers both benefit from financial globalization, as it allows them to access a variety of services and global capital. Consumers have been found to prefer a variety of goods, but they face collective action problems in attempts to organize for or against trade policies. Producers, especially those engaged in international trade, benefit from service liberalization because it gives them access to globally integrated services at competitive prices. The gain is even greater for producers than for individual consumers because financial services liberalization lowers the costs of cross-border financial transactions. Moreover, many consumers do not know that some services firms are foreign, because they often do not differentiate between the nationality of financial firms (e.g., Barclays, HSBC, or ING).

In the absence of public awareness, firms can exert significant influence on policymaking in the sphere of what Culpepper (2010) calls "quiet politics," which is characterized by low political salience and high policy complexity.[66] Due to the technical complexity of services negotiations on behind-the-border regulatory barriers, government negotiators rely on firms to inform them about market access problems around the world. Thus, firms can push for financial globalization in the absence of public or labor opposition.

---

[65] There are concerns about outsourcing service jobs, such as telemarketing or customer service jobs moving to India. The Service Employees International Union joined other labor unions to oppose the Trans-Pacific Partnership. Geishecker and Görg (2013) identified a wage gap between skilled and unskilled labor for offshoring service jobs from the UK.

[66] In this environment, Culpepper (2010) shows that corporate managers utilize three tools: lobbying, working groups, and press framing.

2.5 Alternative Explanations

In this section, I group potential alternative explanations into three categories: international explanations, domestic explanations, and reverse causality (see Table 2.2). International explanations include diffusion, power asymmetry, and external crisis. Domestic explanations include regime type (democracy or autocracy) and party/ideology (left- or right-leaning governments). Reverse causality occurs when the outcome (low regulations) affects the treatment (joining the international agreement).

2.5.1 International Explanations

Power asymmetry. This explanation posits that strong countries advocate for changes that serve their interests.[67] Thus, the outcomes in international negotiations are expected to reflect the interests of the most powerful state in the system—in this case, the United States.

It is beyond dispute that power asymmetry has shaped the trade in financial services negotiations. The US (and its financial firms) wanted financial globalization and sought ways to bring down barriers around the world. Had the US been against multilateral liberalization, the negotiations probably would not have occurred. However, there is an unresolved problem with this explanation: What then explains less than full financial globazliation?

While the US promoted the complete liberalization of financial services, the outcome of the negotiations—countries' liberalization commitments—fell far short of the desired US outcome of full liberalization. If power asymmetry were sufficient, the countries the US pressured the most should have liberalized the most. Yet while the US and EU negotiators spent considerable time and resources pressuring key markets such as Korea, Malaysia, and Brazil, these countries enacted some of the most severe restrictions. The financial services negotiations demonstrate that not even the richest, most

Table 2.2 Alternative Explanations

International Explanations	Domestic Explanations	Reverse Causality
Power asymmetry	Democracy	Low regulations
Diffusion	Party/ideology	
External crisis		

[67] Krasner 1976; Steinberg 2002; Drezner 2008.

powerful country in the world can force global changes in the international economy on its own. Power asymmetry may bring countries to the negotiating table, but it cannot guarantee a desired outcome.

Diffusion. The diffusion argument emphasizes the interdependence of national policy choices, such as countries adopting the economic policies of wealthy countries or neighboring countries that they seek to emulate.[68] This argument would predict the gradual adoption of regulatory reform regionally, then globally. This book shows that it was an international agreement that established an institutional structure in which diffusion occurred contemporaneously.[69] Countries discussed the norms (such as nondiscrimination, independent regulation, and market competition) at the WTO, exchanged ideas, and reached a consensus. They then inscribed these norms and principles into the agreement, which in turn helped guide the domestic regulatory reform that occurred during and after the negotiations.

External crisis. Another popular explanation for financial liberalization is that an external crisis leads to domestic regulatory reform toward liberalization.[70] According to this argument, after a crisis, the government will reform the financial sector to correct a market failure. A financial crisis may also lead countries to open up their financial markets involuntarily in exchange for loans and conditionalities. However, there are two main problems with the crisis explanation: many regulatory reforms have occurred during noncrisis times (e.g., in the early 2000s), and crises can trigger different types of changes. While crises have generally been thought to lead to liberalization, they can also lead to protectionism if the costs are greater than the benefits. For example, the 2007–2008 global financial crisis led to protection policies in developed countries.[71]

2.5.2 Domestic Explanations

Regime type. Many studies of liberalization have found that democracies are more likely to liberalize than autocracies.[72] They have argued that democracy is generally more responsive to public pressure, and that a government is

---

[68] Simmons and Elkins 2004.   [69] Bearce and Bondanella 2007.
[70] Haggard and Maxfield 1996; Martinez-Diaz 2009.   [71] Aggarwal and Evenett 2012.
[72] Przeworski et al. 2000; Milner and Kubota 2005; Eichengreen and Leblang 2008; Jensen et al. 2012.

more likely to enact liberalization policies if the public desires liberalization. However, this argument is not one-directional. If public preferences change, democracies are subject to policy reversals. If the public opposes liberalization, the government may close its doors to imports and foreigners.[73] Indeed, in some democracies, the recent rise of populism has shown a public desire to move away from integration and globalization.[74]

Another reason why democracies may be more likely than nondemocracies to liberalize is that the level of democracy is often correlated with economic development. Many rich countries that liberalize financial services are also democracies, which leads to this empirical pattern. However, whether democratization leads to economic liberalization or vice versa is a long-standing debate in the literature.[75] Since many countries experienced democratization and market liberalization at the same time, it is difficult to establish causality. Moreover, this argument does not explain why nondemocracies liberalize.[76] I test whether democracies have fewer restrictions on their liberalization schedules in Chapter 4.

Party/ideology. Another domestic characteristic that may affect liberalization is the political ideology of the government (or governing party).[77] Right-leaning parties are generally assumed to represent those with capital, and left-leaning parties to speak for labor; the former are thought to be more open to liberalization.[78] This argument has been used to explain cross-country variation as well as within-country change over time.

However, the partisanship argument fails to explain multilateral financial services liberalization for several reasons. First, in this type of financial services liberalization, it is not clear which party would take which position on capital and labor. Services liberalization creates jobs, as it requires MNCs to hire local workers to provide services. Second, the owners of capital and labor in other sectors of the economy benefit from financial services liberalization because it brings in external capital and access to a global market. Third, it is not clear whether (or how) the partisanship argument can explain the decision-making processes across democracies and nondemocracies. Nonetheless, I account for partisanship of the governing party in an analysis reported in Chapter 3.

---

[73] Quinn 2000.   [74] Walter 2021.
[75] Lipset 1959; Rudra 2005; Acemoglu et al. 2019.   [76] Pond 2018.
[77] Garrett 1998; Milner and Judkins 2004; Pinto 2013.   [78] Milner and Judkins 2004.

2.5.3 Reverse Causality

Reverse causality implies that a country's lower regulations motivate it to join an international trade agreement in financial services. It is beyond doubt that the already low regulations in developed countries, especially in the US, helped facilitate negotiations. US firms argued to their government officials that it was unfair for foreign firms to benefit from lower regulations in the US while they could not enjoy reciprocal benefits in foreign countries.

However, most FSA signatories had a high level of regulations before the passage of the FSA (see Chapter 5). Even the US included some restrictions in its liberalization schedule. Moreover, US firms used the threat of multilateral liberalization to further lower domestic regulations in the US, such as the 1999 Financial Modernization Act that repealed the 1933 Glass-Steagall Act. I review the regulatory developments in Chapter 5.

2.6 Scope and Limitations

I study an underexamined but important aspect of financial globalization—how MFCs can establish a commercial presence in foreign countries to facilitate cross-border capital flows. I focus on trade in financial services liberalization, which governs FDI in the financial industry. Examining trade in financial services bridges separate literatures on international trade and finance: trade in financial services liberalization facilitates capital account liberalization, thereby endogenizing foreign capital flows.[79]

The FSA has a broad membership of 102 countries that includes both developed countries and developing countries with virtually no financial services industry. Moreover, financial services are the second-most traded service (18.6%) after distribution services (19.9%).[80] Therefore, it represents an interesting case to unpack the preferences of governments and firms around the world.

The financial industry constitutes a difficult test to explain the global reduction of entry barriers. Given the crucial role that money plays in politics, political leaders have maintained tight control over financial firms. The entry of MFCs can cause the government to lose control in

---

[79] Frieden 1991b; Cohen 1996; Quinn 2003; Mosley 2003. [80] WTO 2019.

44 MAKING FINANCIAL GLOBALIZATION

the strategically and economically important financial industry. This study thus presents a difficult test to examine why countries open their markets to foreign firms.

There are at least two main shortcomings associated with studying the cause and effect of liberalization. The first is the perennial problem that *de jure* liberalization differs from *de facto* liberalization. What countries say they will do may be different from what they actually do in practice. In order to address this gap, I created a new database of domestic financial regulations that examines whether countries complied with this international agreement and implemented domestic regulatory changes. I investigate domestic regulatory changes in Chapter 5 and find that FSA signatories relaxed restrictions in line with the agreement. The second is selection effects: not all countries have joined the FSA, including some WTO members, and those that joined may be different from those that did not join. However, the 102 countries that *did* join accounted for 95% of world trade in financial services.[81] Since these negotiations are not exogenous to countries' preferences, I examine within-country cross-border capital flow changes for those that joined in Chapter 6.

2.7 Conclusion

This chapter proposed a theoretical framework of multilateral lobbying to explain how the multilateral negotiations on financial services liberalization proceeded, from firms facing entry barriers to forming industry coalitions, and governments committing to multilateral liberalization and updating their domestic regulations. It helps explain the process through which MFCs push for the creation of an international agreement. It examines the preferences of main actors in financial globalization—MFCs and governments—and why MFCs would demand an international agreement and governments would engage in fragmented liberalization. It described how financial linkage shapes the demand for (and supply of) financial services liberalization by influencing the preferences of MFCs and governments. Financial linkages within an economy and across countries help identify MFCs' institutional clients, which countries they want to enter, and what services

---

[81] The WTO required a sectoral agreement to cover at least 90% of world trade in the sector.

they will provide abroad. Such linkages push multinational firms to demand and create an international framework to reduce the transaction costs of bilateral bargaining and information asymmetry. Governments liberalized their financial industries to exploit the likely spillover effects in the general economy while protecting their control in the financial sector during liberalization by embedding restrictions.

This framework explains why some countries that do not appear to have a comparative advantage in financial services joined the FSA. Developing countries, even those without active financial markets, joined this international agreement to help domestic firms that *do* enjoy comparative advantages—from agriculture and manufacturing to tourism services industries—access global financial services and capital. Inter-industry financial linkages enabled broad membership of the new international regime in trade in financial services.

However, it would be overreaching to say that an international framework alone causes these domestic regulatory changes. Many governments may have considered (or already implemented) some regulatory reforms. Nevertheless, this framework shows that an international agreement provides the necessary catalyst for contemporaneous regulatory reforms around the world toward implementing the common international regime. It examines the government's delicate balance between maintaining its control in the financial market and generating economic growth from financial services liberalization.

I examine each step of the argument in the following chapters. In Chapter 3, I investigate how financial linkages shape preference formation, coalition formation, and firms' international expansion, using illustrative examples and empirical analyses. In Chapter 4, I discuss the entry barriers faced by MFCs in financial markets around the world and how governments protected SOFIs by embedding restrictions while they were liberalizing multilaterally. In Chapter 5, I test whether countries complied with the international agreement—whether the FSA led to domestic regulatory changes. I also present case studies of regulatory changes in the US and China. In Chapter 6, I assess whether an international economic agreement generates cross-border economic changes. In Chapter 7, I conclude the book by examining the implications of my framework of industry linkages and how it applies to other industries. The concept of industry linkage and the conflict between multinational firms and host governments is not unique to financial services. I discuss how industry linkages can explain other modern international liberalization negotiations on e-commerce or environmental goods. I also identify who the main actors are, what they would like to protect and liberalize, and which countries would be active in negotiations—and why.

3

Financial Linkage and Financial Globalization

This chapter examines why governments, some of which did not even have an active financial market, agreed to open their financial services markets to multinational financial corporations (MFCs). According to the theory of comparative advantages, countries should only seek to liberalize industries in which they have a comparative advantage. Thus, one would expect a financial services liberalization agreement between New York, London, and Tokyo—which together accounted over 75% of international finance at the time—to suffice for financial globalization. However, the World Trade Organization (WTO) Financial Services Agreement (FSA)'s 102 signatories included not only developed countries like the US, Japan, and European Union (EU) members but also developing countries such as Kenya, Lesotho, and Malaysia. Why did countries, even those without comparative advantages in financial services, agree to liberalize their financial markets?

This chapter presents a unifying framework that explains the demand for financial globalization by disaggregating the preferences of main market actors—firms and governments. I argue that financial linkage (the degree to which other firms use financial services in their production of goods and services) can explain the demand side of financial globalization—why firms desire financial globalization and governments open up their financial markets to MFCs' entry. Figure 3.1 illustrates this process. Financial firms expand to other countries to follow their corporate clients, such as commodity and manufacturing firms that expand overseas, and provide cross-border banking, insurance, and securities services for their clients' businesses abroad. However, firms faced entry barriers and incurred transaction costs when negotiating entry into foreign markets. To reduce the barriers to entry and spread norms of liberalization, firms created coalitions by bringing together firms that would benefit from financial globalization—i.e., those that use financial services as inputs. They formed intra-industry and inter-industry coalitions to inform and pressure governments to open up their

Making Financial Globalization: How Firms Shape International Regulatory Cooperation. Clara Park,
Oxford University Press. © Oxford University Press 2025. DOI: 10.1093/oso/9780197761816.003.0003

Figure 3.1 Financial linkage pushes firms and governments.

financial markets. Governments open up their financial markets, despite the costs to these markets, to help industrial firms (especially those engaged in international trade) access global financial services and capital. The entry of MFCs would help industrial firms access global financial services and foreign direct investment (FDI).

The following sections examine these steps in detail. I first explain how to measure financial linkage. I then discuss how financial linkage shapes countries' internationalization strategies by examining MFCs' international expansion patterns and present a case study of Citi's global holdings and regional activities in Africa to analyze how financial linkage shaped the company's international expansion strategy. For the mechanism, I discuss how firms formed industry coalitions across countries and industries to push their liberalization agenda and create an international regime in financial services. Lastly, I show how financial linkages impacted countries' likelihood of joining a multilateral financial liberalization agreement.

3.1 Measuring Financial Linkage

This study builds on an emerging literature in macroeconomics that examines the effects of intersectoral linkages.[1] Financial linkage examines the share of financial inputs in an economy's production of goods and services. Firms in all industries use financial services—such as banking, insurance, and securities services—to some degree. For example, a manufacturing factory borrows from banks to purchase machines and land, and it needs insurance for products and personnel. Thus, measuring the extent to which the financial sector supplies inputs to other industries within the economy

---

[1] Work in this area treats financial linkage as a proxy for the financial sector's role in relation to the rest of the economy: the larger the multiplier, the more central the sector is in the economy (Gabaix 2011; Acemoglu et al. 2012; Fadinger et al. 2015).

FINANCIAL LINKAGE AND FINANCIAL GLOBALIZATION   49

can reveal firms' financial dependence, as well as how these links affect the preferences of firms and the government regarding the liberalization of the financial sector.

I measure countries' financial linkage using a network analysis concept of degree, which is based on the number of links connected to a node.[2] An in-degree indicates the number of links coming into a node, and an out-degree the number of links going out. Analyses of inter-industry networks use sectors as nodes and the flow of intermediate outputs as links. The weighted out-degree, or simply the degree, d_i^{out}, of sector i is the share of i's output in the input supply: w_{ji}.[3] To calculate the out-degree of each country's financial sector, I use the Organisation for Economic Co-operation and Development (OECD) Input-Output Database, which contains 63 countries (27 non-OECD economies, 35 OECD countries). Each economy has 33 industry categories, ranging from agriculture and manufacturing to services. For each country, I calculate the weighted out-degree of the financial industry to other sectors in the economy, or the extent to which its output serves as inputs in other industries, as follows:

$$d_i^{out} = \sum_j^n w_{ji}.$$

(3.1)

I average this calculation over the three years before the final round of FSA negotiations (1995–1997) to obtain smoother estimates. The financial sector's weighted out-degree for each country ranges from 0.5 to 3.5 (Figure 3.2).

Figure 3.3 illustrates the five US sectors with the highest financial linkage (i.e., the financial industry's connectedness within the US economy) during the FSA negotiations. It shows that the finance sector has a high intra-sector linkage (4.61), indicating the depth of financial market activities in the US, followed by real estate activities (1.03). The sectors with the next-highest degree of financial linkage are: renting of machinery and equipment (0.97); other community, social, and personal services (0.90); and health and social work (0.79).[4]

---

[2] Network analysis has been widely used in sociology, political science (Hoff and Ward 2004; Ward et al. 2011; Kinne 2013), and economics (Acemoglu et al. 2012; Fadinger et al. 2015). An emerging literature examines financial firms' networks (Diebold and Yılmaz 2015).

[3] Acemoglu et al. 2012.

[4] These sectors are followed by transport and storage (0.75); electricity, gas, and water supply (0.69); agriculture, hunting, forestry, and fishing (0.57); and research and development and other business activities (0.57).

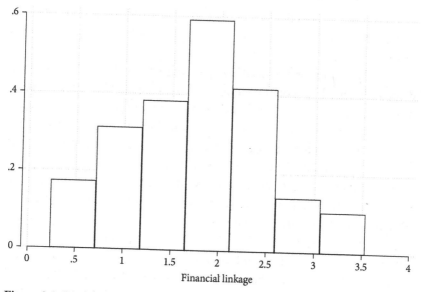

Figure 3.2 Distribution of financial linkage in 63 countries.

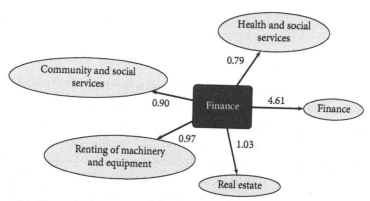

Figure 3.3 Five industries with the highest financial linkage in the US. Measure of industry linkage calculated from the OECD Input-Output Database, 1995–1997 averages.

While rich countries might be assumed to also have a high degree of financial linkage, Figure 3.4 depicts a nonlinear relationship between financial linkage and GDP. The degree of financial linkage is low for the least developed countries (lowest quintile), but it stays around the median at 2 from the second to the highest GDP quintiles. This finding indicates that the financial linkage measure does not simply mirror GDP; rather,

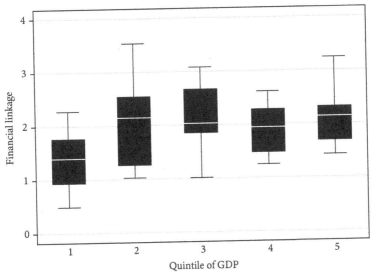

Figure 3.4 Financial linkage by GDP quintile. Financial linkage is not proportional to GDP.

it captures the independent effects of financial linkage that exist at varying levels of development. Moreover, this measure effectively captures an economy's financial dependence better than existing measures of financial development, such as private credit as a share of GDP, and goes beyond the banking sector to include insurance, securities, and other financial services. Thus, it advances the literature on financial development as well as the literature on global value chains by studying industry linkages.

3.2 Impact of Financial Linkage on Financial Firms' International Expansion Strategies

I argue that financial linkage explains MFCs' preferences regarding where they expand internationally (and why). Contrary to the conventional wisdom, financial firms rarely serve ordinary citizens in foreign countries. They instead expand abroad to serve their corporate clients' international expansion. Multinational banks have followed their corporate clients overseas, such as colonies in Latin America and Africa in the nineteenth century, to facilitate their clients' exports and cross-border financial transactions between the home country and the colonies as well as across colonies. For

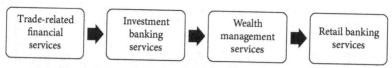

Figure 3.5 Stages of banking business expansion.

example, a UK bank, HSBC, was founded in 1865 by a Scottish businessman who was working for a "large shipping firm" in Hong Kong.[5] The same year, it opened an office in London to "enable exchange operations with China and India," and within 10 years it was financing "the export of tea and silk from China, cotton and jute from India, sugar from the Philippines."[6] Standard Chartered, another UK bank, was created by the merger of two colonial banks—the Standard Bank, which was founded in South Africa to facilitate the diamond trade, and the Chartered Bank, which helped cotton, sugar, and tobacco exporters in colonial India and Indonesia.[7] Multinational corporations (MNCs) benefit from having their main bank handle cross-border financial services to avoid the transaction costs associated with using multiple providers. Therefore, MFCs follow their corporate clients to provide cross-border financial services.[8]

To analyze financial firms' international expansion patterns, I examined the global operations of five international banks with a wide geographic scope: Citi, Bank of America, HSBC, JPMorgan Chase, and Standard Chartered.[9] I find that multinational banks expand in four main phases, based on their degree of financial linkage: (1) trade-related financial services, (2) commercial and investment banking services, (3) wealth management, and (4) retail banking.

Figure 3.5 illustrates how financial linkage shapes MFCs' entry into host countries, from serving institutional clients to retail customers.[10] My analysis finds that trade-related cross-border financial services are the most common line of business for financial firms' global offices. Exporters and importers

---

[5] HSBC History Timeline, https://www.hsbc.com/who-we-are/our-history/history-timeline.
[6] HSBC History Timeline, https://www.hsbc.com/who-we-are/our-history/history-timeline.
[7] The Standard Bank of British South Africa and the Chartered Bank of India, Australia, and China were founded in 1853 and 1862, respectively. For a history of Standard Chartered, see Cope 1987 and *The Guardian*, "Standard Chartered: A Short History," August 7, 2012.
[8] J.P. Morgan, Treasury Services, https://www.jpmorgan.com/global.
[9] I chose these five banks because they had a presence in all five continents. Some firms have a narrower geographic scope than others, but in the countries in which they operate, they have similar phases of foreign expansion.
[10] While the order may vary depending on a firm's main business, many MFCs have expanded using this pattern.

alike benefit from seamless financial transactions during international trade, as they cross multiple borders and need financing across borders. MFCs facilitate international trade by providing trade-related financial services across borders, including writing letters of credit and insuring products in transit.

The second phase of financial internationalization is commercial and investment banking services. Depending on a host country's level of economic and financial development, MFCs can advise on mergers and acquisitions or initial public offerings in host markets. For example, Citi's 98 international offices all first offered commercial banking services for corporate clients; none of these offices initially offered retail services. In fact, only about 20% of them offered retail services at all. For example, Citi Nigeria states that its business in Nigeria is to help "Nigerian customers looking to expand their businesses beyond the shores of the country" and "raise capital by tapping into international capital markets."[11] Similarly, J.P. Morgan Chase only offers institutional banking services abroad to "corporations, governments, wealthy individuals and institutional investors," and it offers no retail services.[12] Bank of America also does not have a retail business outside the US.[13]

The third common phase of financial internationalization is asset (wealth) management services for wealthy individuals and enterprises. In a growing economy, a substantial number of prosperous individuals and enterprises emerge that seek help managing their assets and investments. Affluent individuals, such as business leaders and state-owned enterprise (SOE) managers, may move their money to foreign financial firms, especially if they already do business in other countries or send their children abroad to study. Some MFCs offer such services in markets with a growing number of wealthy individuals to manage and advise investments at home and abroad. They can provide their know-how in private banking services and wealth management across borders.

The last step of financial expansion (and the least common business) for foreign banks in host countries is retail banking.[14] For example, HSBC South

---

[11] Citi website, "Countries and Jurisdictions: Nigeria," https://www.citigroup.com/citi/about/countries-and-jurisdictions/nigeria.html.

[12] JPMorgan Chase website, "Our Business," https://www.jpmorganchase.com/about/our-business.

[13] In other countries, Bank of America only provides commercial banking services through the former Merrill Lynch business it acquired during the 2008 global financial crisis.

[14] Two foreign banks with a huge retail presence in Africa are headquartered in former colonizing countries: France's Société Générale and the UK's Standard Chartered. The latter acquired the Bank of West Africa, formerly the Bank of British West Africa.

54 MAKING FINANCIAL GLOBALIZATION

Africa states that it "does not provide any services to retail and personal banking clients," and it emphasizes that its branches are for "corporate customers only, and we unfortunately do not have any ability to support Personal Banking customers with personal banking matters such as cash, ATM [automated teller machine] services."[15] They instead list local partner banks from which customers can withdraw cash abroad.[16]

There are three main reasons why retail banking is the last and least common business for banks operating in foreign countries. First, retail banking involves higher regulatory costs than commercial banking. Since governments want to reduce the risk of bank runs and the resulting instability, they enforce tougher restrictions on retail banking to protect individual depositors.[17] Second, state-owned or private domestic banks often dominate retail banking networks with their local advantages, and as a result competition against entrenched incumbents is fierce. Managers of domestic banks, many of whom have close ties to politicians, pressure their home governments to block or obstruct foreign entry into retail banking. Third, retail banking requires large initial sunk costs, which the potential revenues from individual clients may not offset. Setting up branches throughout a country is expensive, since it involves leasing buildings, hiring personnel (such as bank tellers), and installing and maintaining ATMs. These large costs have pushed some banks to close or sell off retail business during economic downturns. For example, after the global financial crisis, Citi sold its consumer franchise in Belgium to Crédit Mutuel Nord Europe,[18] and Barclays sold off its retail business in Africa to a South African bank, Absa, "completing its exit from a more than 90-year presence on the continent".[19]

Retail banking is thus less attractive to MFCs, and they expand abroad mainly to serve corporate clients through financial linkages. This analysis demonstrates that financial linkage to other industries drives financial firms' internationalization strategies. MFCs expand abroad to provide their corporate clients with trade-related cross-border financial services. If host countries have further financial opportunities, MFCs seek to provide more

---

[15] HSBC in South Africa website, https://www.about.hsbc.co.za/hsbc-in-africa.

[16] Bank of America, "Find International ATM Partners," https://locators.bankofamerica.com/international.html.

[17] For example, the US Federal Deposit Insurance Corporation guarantees individuals' deposits up to $250,000.

[18] Reuters, "Citigroup to Sell Belgian Retail Business to CMNE," December 28, 2011.

[19] L. White, "Barclays announces sale of remaining shares in South Africa's Absa," Reuters, August 31, 2022.

business, such as investment banking and wealth management services for firms and wealthy individuals. In some countries, they also offer retail banking services to retail customers. The next section further examines the role of financial linkage in MFCs' international expansion through a case study of Citibank to understand their preferences in financial globalization.

3.2.1 Citi's International Expansion Strategies

This section investigates how financial linkage affects MFCs' preferences related to (and strategies employed in) international expansion. I examine Citibank because it played a key role in creating the FSA, along with AIG and American Express.[20] I analyze Citi's financial linkage to other firms, industries, and countries to explore how such ties shaped its foreign expansion strategy. Since its client list is proprietary information, I utilize Citi's publicly listed investments as filed with the US Securities and Exchange Commission in its quarterly and annual reports and the Thompson 13F database to evaluate its institutional holdings and international offices.[21]

Table 3.1 presents Citi's top investments by country and industry before the FSA from 1995 to 1997. Citi enjoyed wide international coverage, from Canada and France to China and Mexico. It invested in a variety of industries; the two most prominent were oil and gas extraction (Canada and France) and primary metal industries (Argentina). The next two largest investments were in services industries: communications in Luxembourg and insurance carriers in Switzerland, followed by the Chinese electronics industry.[22]

Table 3.2 reports Citi's investments at the firm level at the time of the FSA negotiations. Citi invested in industrial conglomerates such as consumer goods (Johnson & Johnson, Coca Cola, 3M, GE, and GM) as well as the pharmaceutical (Merck) and oil and mining industries (Schlumberger and Atlantic Richfield). The list also includes IBM and Travelers Insurance,

---

[20] Freeman 2000.

[21] The 10K is an annual report pursuant to Section 13 or 15(d) of the Securities Exchange Act of 1934. Investors in the stock market also assess these reports to find out about a firm's investments as well as its executives' stock trading. The 13F data comes from the Thompson/Refinitive Database.

[22] The countries that follow (not shown) are Brazil's communications and electric and gas industries, as well as the communications industries in Hong Kong and China.

56 MAKING FINANCIAL GLOBALIZATION

Table 3.1 Citi's Investment by Country, Amount, and Industry, 1995–1997

Country	Investment ($Mil.)	Industry
Canada	90.9	Oil and gas extraction
France	88.1	Oil and gas extraction
Argentina	67.9	Primary metal industries
Luxembourg	58	Communications
Switzerland	51.7	Insurance carriers
China	47.7	Electronics and other electrical equipment
Bermuda	42.8	Business services
Switzerland	42.1	Oil and gas extraction
Finland	35.3	Electronic & other electrical equipment
Bermuda	34.7	Hotels and other lodgings
UK	32.6	Communications
Ireland	31.7	Electronic and other electrical equipment
Mexico	29.9	Transportation by air

Source: Author's calculations based on data from the Thompson 13F database.

Table 3.2 Citi's 15 Largest Invested Firms, 1995–1997 ($ Millions)

Firm	Industry	Investment
Travelers Group	Insurance	679
IBM	IT	249
GE	Manufacturing	248
Philip Morris	Tobacco	178
Lockheed Martin	Defense manufacturing	177
Merck & Co	Pharmaceutical	171
Exxon	Oil and gas	149
Johnson & Johnson	Manufacturing	119
3M	Manufacturing	118
Amoco	Oil and gas	116
Tenneco	Manufacturing	107
Coca Cola	Beverages	105
GTE	Telecommunications	89
AT&T	Telecommunications	88
Schlumberger	Oil and gas	88

Source: Author's calculations based on data from the Thompson 13F database.

which it later acquired, and American Express.[23] Citi thus invests far and wide and in different industries.

Next, I use an illustrative example of Citi's foreign expansion in a developing country in Africa (Ghana) to closely examine how financial linkage

---

[23] Citi's acquisition of Travelers is significant for this study because it also accelerated a change in domestic regulation, which I discuss in Chapter 5.

3.2.2 Financial Linkage and Citi's Expansion in Ghana

This section provides an in-depth examination of why MFCs expand overseas, especially to developing countries with small financial markets. Africa has traditionally had legacy foreign banks from colonial times, when banks followed traders to their colonies: British banks such as Standard Chartered and Barclays, French banks such as BNP Paribas and Société Générale, and Spanish banks such as Santander and BBVA had established footholds in their respective former colonies. Ghana, a former British colony, even had the Bank of British West Africa double as its central bank during the colonial period until its independence in 1953.[24] Even after independence, foreign banks continued to enter Africa, following their MNC clients.

Citi entered Ghana in 2003, which at the time had a GDP per capita of $373, along with 17 other African countries with similar low per capita GDPs.[25] It is puzzling why Citi would enter countries with low levels of economic and financial development. I argue that financial linkage shaped Citi's decisions to enter these countries to facilitate its MNC clients' trade and investments. In fact, Citi has no retail business in Africa. Instead, it provides "investment banking services and corporate finance deals for selected clients" in Ghana, such as MNCs and government entities, including SOEs.[26]

Citi serves MNCs and SOEs in industries in which Ghana has comparative advantages, such as gold, cocoa, and oil. An aide to the country's vice president stated that Citi, even before its full entry to Ghana, "for the past 10 years has been engaged in the financing of operations of the Ghana Cocoa Board [Ghana's Cocoa SOE], Volta River Authority [Ghana's power generation SOE], and the oil and gas industry."[27]

---

[24] Austin and Uche 2007; Standard Chartered, "About Us," https://www.sc.com/gh/about-us/.

[25] Ghana's per capita GDP has remained below $400 since its independence (World Bank's World Development Indicator). These 17 countries are Algeria, Cameroon, Democratic Republic of Congo (DRC), Egypt, Gabon, Ghana, Ivory Coast, Kenya, Morocco, Nigeria, Qatar, Senegal, South Africa, Tanzania, Tunisia, Uganda, and Zambia. The only other bank with broad geographic coverage in Africa is Standard Chartered, which has established a banking presence in the continent's former British colonies.

[26] Citi website, "Citi Countries and Jurisdictions: Ghana," https://www.citigroup.com/citi/about/countries-and-jurisdictions/ghana.html.

[27] *Ghana Web*, "U.S. Citi Bank to Start Operations in Ghana," March 5, 2013.

58 MAKING FINANCIAL GLOBALIZATION

Citi serves Ghana's cocoa industry—the country's second-largest export. The government controls the industry through its SOE, the Cocoa Board of Ghana (Cocobod), which buys cocoa beans in advance to provide a stable financial environment for cocoa farmers.[28] The government borrows money from international banks to make these payments, and Citi has arranged loans for Cocobod with other banks.[29] For instance, in 1997 Citibank and the Ghana Agricultural Development Bank arranged an international syndicate of 35 banks to secure a $275 million loan to help Cocobod purchase cocoa in advance.[30] Since then, Cocobod has borrowed between $200 million and $1.1 billion a year from an international syndicate of 20–30 banks, including Citi, to finance its cocoa purchases.[31]

Citi also helps MNCs and the state-owned oil company, Ghana National Petroleum Corporation, sell oil internationally.[32] Following the discovery of a large quantity of oil at the Jubilee field in 2007, oil MNCs from all over the world flocked to Ghana.[33] MFCs, including Citi, Standard Chartered, Barclays, and Goldman Sachs,[34] have advised oil MNCs on acquiring stakes in the Jubilee oil field through their commercial and investment banking services. In the gold and diamond industry, Citi also handles all payments for gold and diamonds through the country's main mining SOE, the Precious Minerals Marketing Company (PMMC).[35] The PMMC informs foreign investors that "payments for gold and diamonds are made through Precious Minerals Marketing Company by bank transfers from Citibank, New York, to the [b]ank of Ghana (i.e., the central bank of Ghana)."[36]

In addition to working through SOEs, the Ghanaian government has also received direct financing from Citi, which was the first bank to manage the government's international bond sale (Eurobonds) in 2007, which raised

[28] Reuters, "UPDATE 1-Ghana Abandons Plan To Cut Cocoa Farmers' Prices," March 28, 2018.
[29] Panafrican News Agency (Dakar), "Ghana: Cocoa Board Clinches 275-Million-Dollar Deal." October 14, 1997.
[30] Panafrican News Agency (Dakar), "Ghana: Cocoa Board Clinches 275-Million-Dollar Deal," October 14, 1997.
[31] Ghana Cocoa Board, "Cocobod Signs US $1.13 Billion Trade Finance Facility for 2022/2023 Cocoa Season," October 4, 2022.
[32] Kwasi Kpodo, "Ghana Hedging Oil Output at $107/Barrel: finmin," Reuters, June 9, 2011.
[33] The government granted entry to the following MNCs: Tullow Oil (UK), Kosmos Energy (US), Anadarko (US), Petro SA (South Africa), ENI SpA (Italy), and Vitol (Netherlands). BP, Shell, Exxon, China's CNOC, and India's Oil and Natural Gas Corporation bid unsuccessfully.
[34] Joseph Chaney and Narayanan Somasundaram, "ONGC Taps Citi for Kosmos Ghana Stake Bid: Sources," Reuters, July 20, 2009.
[35] Precious Minerals Marketing Company History, https://www.pmmc.gov.gh/pmmc/about/history.
[36] International Business Publications 2015, p. 80.

$750 million.[37] Ghana has since issued seven more Eurobond sales, of which Citi handled six, to meet its debt obligations and fund infrastructure projects.[38] Citi has provided extensive financial services—including treasury services, loans, and IPOs—for corporate and institutional clients in Ghana, such as MNCs and SOEs, without entering the retail market.

Citi also operates in other African countries, including Gabon, Kenya, Nigeria, and Zambia. In Keyna and Nigeria, Citi has also managed Eurobond sales.[39] In Kenya, Citi also serves multiple industries, including aviation, shipping, power, energy, manufacturing, and infrastructure.[40] In Gabon, Citi serves oil firms—it has two branches in the country, one in the capital, Libreville, and the other in Port-Gentil, "where oil activities are concentrated."[41] Similarly, in Zambia, Citi services foreign and domestic firms in the copper industry by operating two branches, one in the capital and another in the "copper belt."[42] Citi's activities in Africa show that financial firms expand abroad to serve their MNC clients. Governments allow foreign financial firms to enter their markets and help industries in which they have comparative advantages.

3.3 A Quantitative Analysis of Financial Linkage and Financial Globalization

In this section, I provide a quantitative analysis of how financial linkage affected countries' variation in financial globalization. I argued that a government is more likely to liberalize its financial market if the economy has a high degree of financial linkage (i.e., if its industries depend heavily on financial services for their production), which will help industrial firms access

---

[37] Eurobonds are bonds issued in any foreign currency. They are not necessarily European bonds, and are not sold only on the European market.

[38] Oxford Business Group, "What Will Ghana Do with Its $3bn Eurobond?," February 25, 2020. Other foreign banks, such as Standard Chartered, JP Morgan, Bank of America, and UBS, have also helped Ghana lead Eurobond sales. Bloomberg, "Ghana Is Said to Name Citi, Three Others to Market Eurobond," March 20, 2018.

[39] D. Miriri, "Kenya to Pick Citi, JPMorgan to Advise on Eurobond Sale," Reuters, February 7, 2018. C. Ohuocha, "Nigeria Union Bank Working with Citi on Eurobond, Others to Follow—Sources," Reuters, March 1, 2018.

[40] Citibank N.A. (Kenya Branches) Annual Report and Financial Statements, December 31, 2018, https://tinyurl.com/4zwkcuz8.

[41] Citi Countries and Jurisdictions: Gabon, https://www.citigroup.com/citi/about/countries-and-jurisdictions/gabon.html.

[42] Citi Countries and Jurisdictions: Zambia, https://www.citigroup.com/citi/about/countries-and-jurisdictions/zambia.html.

60 MAKING FINANCIAL GLOBALIZATION

foreign capital and financial services. I thus hypothesized that if a country's industries are heavily dependent on the financial industry, as measured by high levels of financial linkage, it is more likely to join the FSA. I examine this prediction using a country's financial linkage and FSA membership.

To study the relationship between a country's financial linkage and probability of signing the FSA, I estimate (i) a series of logit models that adjust for different sets of confounders (i.e., making a selection-on-observables assumption for inference) and (ii) optimal full matching analysis (Hansen, 2004). The dependent variable is an indicator that equals 1 if a country joined the FSA, and 0 otherwise.[43] All model specifications employ heteroskedasticity-consistent standard errors.

Prior research provides two economic and political explanations of why countries would sign an international liberalization agreement in financial services. The first economic explanation is that rich countries are more likely to sign such an agreement because their firms are already doing well internationally. However, least developed countries such as Gabon, Guyana, and Niger also joined the FSA, challenging the wealth-based explanation. The second economic explanation is that countries that already have a high share of foreign banks or FDI inflows are likely to join the FSA to further increase their foreign capital inflows. I control for these explanations—economy size and foreign exposure—by including data on GDP per capita, population size, exports, foreign bank share, and FDI inflows from the World Bank's World Development Indicators database.

The first political explanation relates to the characteristics of regime types: many studies have argued that democracies are more likely to join international agreements than autocracies[44] because of their liberal values[45] or the median voter's preference for liberalization.[46] For these reasons, a country's level of democracy may determine its probability of signing the FSA. I therefore include each country's Polity IV score to indicate its level of democracy on a scale from −10 (less democratic) to +10 (more democratic). The second political explanation is that countries with well-developed property rights may be more likely to join because they will have a more hospitable environment for foreign investment. I therefore also include

---

[43] Since I am dealing with a limited dependent variable and a small sample size, I employ the biased-reduction generalized linear model (GLM) estimator suggested by Kosmidis and Firth (2009). The Online Appendix displays the results using a standard logit model.

[44] Mansfield et al. 2002.   [45] Bliss and Russett 1998.

[46] For instance, median voters are likely to benefit from liberalization as consumers (Baker, 2005).

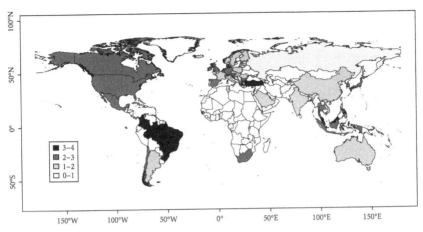

Figure 3.6 Financial linkage around the world.

a measure of property rights guaranteed by the government, which ranges from 0 (weaker) to 1 (stronger) from La Porta et al. (2002).

Figure 3.6 depicts the degree of financial linkage around the world and shows which countries are included in our sample. The highest degree of financial linkage (blue) is found in medium-sized economies, such as Brazil, Colombia, Malaysia, Thailand, and Turkey.[47] The next-highest tier (green) includes some rich countries, such as the US and Canada, as well as emerging economies, such as China, India, and South Africa. The third tier (yellow) contains countries with less diversified economies, such as Australia, Luxembourg, Russia, Taiwan, and Vietnam. Our data set is missing input-output data for many countries in Africa (white). While 102 countries joined the FSA, we only have data for the main explanatory variable, financial linkage, for 60 countries.[48] The measure of financial linkage, using the OECD Input-Output Database, has limited coverage, although it provides the preferred high-quality measure of financial linkage. As an alternative measure, I employ *Domestic Credit to the Private Sector*, commonly used in international finance studies to proxy for the level of *banking* integration. It only measures bank loans and does not include other financial services, such as insurance and securities. While it underestimates industry dependence on the financial industry, it increases the sample size to 130 countries.[49] In the robustness section, I show that an alternative measure of financial linkage

---

[47] The highest tier is from 2 to 3.1 because the highest linkage is Malaysia's at 3.03.
[48] OECD Input-Output Database.   [49] IMF International Financial Statistics.

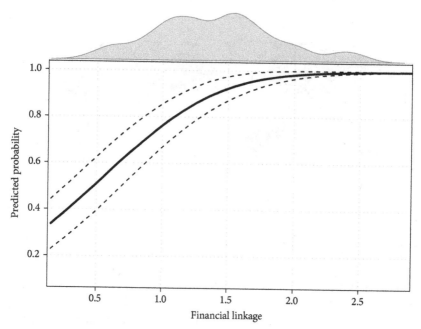

Figure 3.7 Probability of signing the FSA as a function of financial linkage. Predicted probabilities with robust 95% Confidence Interval. All other variables held at observed values. The sample distribution of financial linkage is shown via a kernel density plot (bandwidth 0.15) on top of the plot.

that encompasses the African continent produces comparable substantive results, though it only covers the banking sector.

3.3.1 Results

This analysis demonstrates that financial linkage has a positive and statistically significant effect on countries' likelihood of joining the FSA across all specifications. Figure 3.7 displays the probability of FSA signing as a function of financial linkage using Specification (3) from Table 3.3. For example, an increase in financial linkage from 1.47 to 1.80 (an approximate shift from the median to the 75th percentile) is akin to moving from South Africa's level of financial linkage to that of Spain and Belgium.

FINANCIAL LINKAGE AND FINANCIAL GLOBALIZATION 63

Table 3.3 Marginal Effect of Financial Linkage on Probability of FSA Signing

	(1)	(2)	(3)	(4)	(5)
Financial Linkages	0.216***	0.231***	0.214***	0.241***	0.199***
	(0.054)	(0.062)	(0.027)	(0.030)	(0.031)
GDP per capita (PPP)	0.051***	0.054**	0.047**	0.052**	0.035*
	(0.014)	(0.019)	(0.015)	(0.016)	(0.017)
FDI Inflows		0.008	0.008	0.009	0.017*
		(0.016)	(0.008)	(0.009)	(0.007)
Exports		−0.001	−0.003***	−0.003***	−0.003***
		(0.001)	(0.001)	(0.001)	(0.001)
Foreign Bank Share			0.051***	0.055***	0.043***
			(0.009)	(0.010)	(0.007)
RCA				−0.006	−0.006
				(0.007)	(0.006)
Polity					0.008*
					(0.004)
Property Rights					0.024
					(0.024)
N	60	56	55	51	48

Note: Entries are marginal effects calculated from a series of logit models estimated using the bias-reduced estimator of Kosmidis and Firth (2009). Robust standard errors in parentheses. All inputs standardized to mean zero and unit standard deviation.

Table 3.3 reports the average marginal effects for different model specifications with financial linkage scaled to have a mean of zero with unit standard deviation. Specification (1) only adjusts for the level of economic development (GDP per capita adjusted for purchasing power parity) and finds that a one-standard-deviation increase in financial linkage corresponds to a 21.6-percentage-point increase in the probability of signing the FSA. Specification (2) adds controls for additional economic factors, such as the size of FDI inflows and that exports as a share of GDP, since countries that already receive a high level of FDI inflows or that export actively may be more likely to liberalize their financial services industries. Controlling for these does not change the result. A country's share of foreign banks may also make it more likely to join the FSA to facilitate the financial services that these foreign banks already provide. Thus, Specification (3) controls

64 MAKING FINANCIAL GLOBALIZATION

for the share of foreign banks[50] and finds that it is positively associated with a country's likelihood of joining the FSA. However, the effect of financial linkage stays about the same (21.4-percentage-point increase).

Specification (4) tests the conventional explanation—that countries with comparative advantages are expected to liberalize—using Balassa's (1965) measure of revealed comparative advantages in financial services. I find that financial linkage predicts the probability of joining the FSA, while a country's comparative advantage in financial services does not have a statistically significant effect on its likelihood of joining the FSA. Finally, Specification (5) controls for political factors such as regime type and property rights protection, since I expect countries that are more democratic (higher Polity scores) and those with strong property rights protection to be more likely to sign the FSA. I find that even after accounting for political variables, the effects of financial linkage remain at around a 20-percentage-point increase in the probability of signing the FSA. In sum, the evidence presented here corroborates that financial linkage affects countries' probability of joining the FSA.

3.3.2 Optimal Matching Analysis

A key issue associated with gauging how financial linkage affected FSA membership using observational cross-section data is the role of confounding variables that both influence a country's likelihood of joining *and* affect its level of financial linkage. In other words, countries with "high" and "low" levels of linkage may differ systematically in characteristics that also affect their probability of joining the FSA, such as GDP or export orientation. To address this concern, I "preprocess" my data so that countries that are "treated" with a high degree of financial linkage are comparable in terms of covariates to the "control" group with low financial linkage (Ho et al. 2007). While matching and regression both make a selection-on-observables assumption, matching relaxes functional form assumptions about the covariates in the matching stage (Sekhon 2009).

I define countries as belonging to the high-linkage "treatment" group when they are above the 0.7 quantile (or about 1.8 in financial linkage)

---

[50] Foreign bank share has two countries in the sample that have zero values, so I took a square root of the value instead of dropping them.

FINANCIAL LINKAGE AND FINANCIAL GLOBALIZATION 65

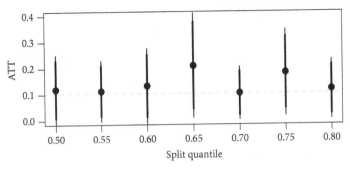

Figure 3.8 Average treatment effects at varying split quantiles. Shown are estimated average treatment effects on the treated (with 90 and 95% confidence intervals) using different quantiles to define treatment.

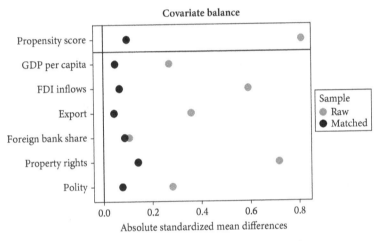

Figure 3.9 Covariate balance plot of raw and matched sample.

of the financial linkage distribution. Figure 3.8 demonstrates that different cutoffs do not substantially alter the results. I employ optimal full matching to balance covariates with the smallest absolute mean distance (Hansen 2004). There are 36 countries in the control group and 16 in the treatment group. The covariate balance plot (Figure 3.9) indicates that the balance improves significantly after matching. For example, the mean difference between treated and untreated countries for FDI inflows and property rights is halved. Foreign bank share was relatively well balanced even before matching. As a summary measure, the propensity score also declined substantially after matching.

66 MAKING FINANCIAL GLOBALIZATION

Table 3.4 Average Treatment Effect on the Treated (ATT) of High Financial Linkage on the Probability of Signing the FSA

	Model 1	Model 2
Treatment Effect	0.104*	0.126*
	(0.051)	(0.052)
Controls	No	Yes
N	52	52

Note: Cluster-robust standard errors, clustered by matching subclass.

With these preprocessed matched data, I estimate the average treatment effects for the treatment group (Table 3.4). Using the matched sample, countries with a high degree of financial linkage are 10.4 percentage points more likely to join the FSA. Specification (2) includes covariates to capture any remaining imbalances after matching. When combined with covariates, financial linkage increases a country's likelihood of joining the FSA by 12.6 percentage points. Both results are statistically significant at the 99% level. The Ordinary Least Squares (OLS) and matching results thus demonstrate that a high degree of financial linkage increases countries' probability of signing the FSA. Countries with industries that depend on financial services inputs are more likely to join to help their domestic firms access global financial services and capital.

3.3.3 Robustness Checks

I test a set of alternative explanations that may influence liberalization and financial linkage intensity. Table 3.5 reports marginal effects with robust standard errors. I explain each set of tests below.

(1) Political partisanship. A country's political partisanship may affect its likelihood of joining an international liberalization agreement. Previous work in the literature on trade and domestic politics has argued that left-leaning governments are more likely to have anti-trade and anti-liberalization attitudes and that right-leaning parties are likely to be open to liberalization.[51] However, prior studies have found that political partisanship has mixed effects on financial liberalization.[52] Using the Inter-American

---

[51] Garrett 1998; Milner and Judkins 2004; Pinto 2013. [52] Quinn and Inclan 1997.

Table 3.5 Robustness Checks

	Mfx	SE	N
(1) Partisanship of government	0.175	(0.054)	47
(2) Asian financial crisis	0.220	(0.033)	50
(3) Tax haven countries	0.214	(0.027)	55
(4) World region FE	0.264	(0.028)	55
(5) Five-year average values	0.216	(0.029)	55
(6) Economy size (total GDP)	0.260	(0.036)	55
(7) Intra-industry financial linkage	0.155	(0.023)	55
(8) Free market ideology	0.209	(0.054)	39
(9) Alternative measure of financial linkage	0.431	(0.118)	130

Note: Based on Specification (3) in Table 3.3. Marginal effects with robust standard errors in parentheses.

Bank's Database of Political Institutions,[53] I include indicator variables for the partisanship of the government and find that it does not affect the likelihood of joining the FSA. Even accounting for political partisanship, the effects of financial linkage increase the probability of joining the FSA by 17.5 percentage points.

(2) Asian financial crisis. The 1997 crisis, which occurred during the FSA negotiations, may have influenced the likelihood of joining the agreement for countries that were directly and indirectly affected by it. The crisis could have made affected countries either less likely to join the agreement (to keep out foreign financial firms) or more likely to join it (to attract foreign capital that had fled). I control for the indicator of IMF loan recipients, such as Korea, Indonesia, and Thailand, and countries that were severely affected by the crisis, such as Hong Kong, Malaysia, and the Philippines. Controlling for countries affected by the Asian Financial Crisis leaves the estimates virtually unchanged.

(3) Tax haven countries. A country's tax haven status may make it more likely to join an international liberalization agreement. Tax havens have favorable tax conditions that allow multinational firms and wealthy individuals to evade taxes in their home countries; these countries generally rely on the financial sector for economic growth. Since financial services is their comparative advantage, tax havens may be more likely to join the liberalization agreement. My sample of countries includes six tax havens;[54]

---

[53] Cruz et al. 2018.
[54] The tax haven countries in the sample are Antigua and Barbuda, Aruba, Barbados, Cyprus, Malta, and Mauritius OECD, *The Global Forum on Transparency and Exchange of Information for Tax Purposes*, 2012.

68 MAKING FINANCIAL GLOBALIZATION

including an indicator for tax havens in the model leaves the marginal effect of financial linkage virtually unchanged.

(4) Region fixed effects. I include region fixed effects to control for region-specific differences. The estimates indicate that financial linkage boosts the likelihood of joining the FSA by 26.4 percentage points.

(5) Longer pre-treaty window. I extend the pre-treaty window for covariates from 3 years (1995–1997) to 5-year averages (1993–1997) and find that the results remain substantively the same.

(6) GDP. For an alternative measure of GDP, I control for total (rather than per capita) GDP to measure the total size of the economy and find that the effect of financial linkage is essentially unchanged (26-percentage-point increase).

(7) Intra-industry financial linkage. I have examined inter-industry financial linkage in the main analysis and excluded intra-industry ties within the financial industry because they would skew the results toward financially developed countries. I test to see if including intra-industry linkage changes my results as a robustness check. I find only a slight reduction in the estimated effect size. A one-unit decrease in financial linkage is associated with a 15.5-percentage-point increase in the probability of FSA membership. This effect is statistically different from zero.

(8) Free market ideology. Countries that adhere to a free market ideology may be more likely to join the FSA. I use data from the Manifesto Project that examines parties' policy positions in 50 countries.[55] I examine parties' preferences for a free market economy (as indicated by mentions of laissez-faire economics and private property rights in their manifestos). Because the data only covers 50 countries, the overlap with the OECD Input-Output Database is small, yielding a sample size of 39 countries. Nevertheless, including the variable for free market ideology does not change the results significantly.

(9) Alternative measure of financial linkage. Using an alternative measure of financial linkage–domestic credit to the private sector–yields an estimated increase of 43.1 percentage points, indicating that financial linkage, however measured, makes countries more likely to join the FSA.

The results so far have demonstrated that financial linkage motivates countries to open up their markets to foreign financial services providers. Governments are more likely to liberalize financial services when their firms

---

[55] Lehmann et al. 2017.

depend on such services for inputs and would benefit from the entry of foreign providers.

3.4 Conclusion

This chapter introduced a unified framework to understand the sources of the preferences of MFCs and governments in financial globalization. It analyzed how financial linkage—firms' dependence on the financial industry for inputs—shaped firms' industry coalitions and governments' decisions to liberalize their financial markets even in countries that do not have comparative advantages in financial services. Such linkages brought firms together to create within- and across-industry coalitions to push for a worldwide liberalization in financial services.

Firms engaged in a multilateral lobbying campaign to push home governments, host governments, and international organizations concurrently. The case studies of multinational banks' expansion strategies and the FSA negotiations highlighted the preferences and strategies of MFCs and governments in financial globalization. The study of Citibank in Ghana and other African countries showed why MFCs expand overseas. The quantitative analysis demonstrated that countries with a greater degree of financial linkage were more likely to join the FSA.

4

Fragmented Liberalization in the Financial Industry

This chapter examines the second step of the puzzle: why governments joined the Financial Services Agreement (FSA) but incorporated restrictions to limit multinational financial corporations' (MFCs') entry, such as those related to the type of ownership (majority or minority), type of enterprise (i.e., branches, subsidiaries, wholly owned enterprises), and personnel—leading to *fragmented liberalization*. For example, countries included various restrictions including which cities foreign financial firms can first enter (China), how many members of the board of directors must hold citizenship (US), and what type of foreign financial firms can operate (Korea). Even close neighbors varied in their level of liberalization. For example, Mozambique did not restrict foreign entry in banking, but its neighbor Zimbabwe set a ceiling of foreign equity participation up to 60%.[1]

Figure 4.1 shows the distribution of financial trade restrictions in the FSA. The BRICS countries (Brazil, Russia, India, China, and South Africa) all fall into the highest band of restrictions, whereas Angola, Australia, and Japan are in the lowest band. The US, which as the world leader in finance is expected to have few restrictions, is surprisingly in the middle. What explains this fragmented liberalization?

Prior work on liberalization has examined political *or* economic factors, such as regime type and partisan politics or the level of economic or financial development. Some studies argue that democracies are more likely to liberalize than nondemocracies due to their liberal values or the median voter's preferences for liberalization.[2] Some work in this area examines variations within democracies and argues that right-leaning parties, backed by capital owners, are more likely to liberalize than left-leaning parties,[3] while others

---

[1] For more detailed information, see the World Trade Organization (WTO) FSA schedules of the US (GATS/SC/90/Suppl. 3), China (GATS/SC/135), Korea (GATS/SC/48/Suppl. 3), Mozambique (GATS/SC/54), and Zimbabwe (GATS/SC/94).

[2] Quinn and Toyoda 2007; Menaldo and Yoo 2015.   [3] Garrett 1998.

Making Financial Globalization: How Firms Shape International Regulatory Cooperation. Clara Park,
Oxford University Press. © Oxford University Press 2025. DOI: 10.1093/oso/9780197761816.003.0004

FRAGMENTED LIBERALIZATION IN THE FINANCIAL INDUSTRY 71

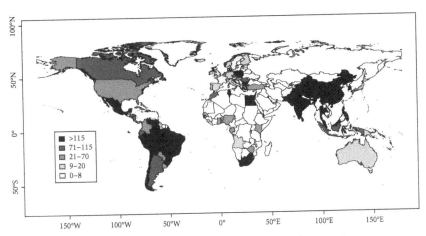

Figure 4.1 Total number of financial trade restrictions, by country.

find that partisanship has ambiguous effects on liberalization.[4] According to economic explanations, such as the theory of comparative advantage, rich or more financially developed countries are more likely to liberalize than their less economically and financially developed counterparts. However, these studies fail to adequately explain the variation in liberalization among democracies or among similar-sized economies, such as why some democracies close their insurance market or only permit 30% foreign ownership, or why the US, Japan, and the European Union (EU) have pursued different types of liberalization. Examining political or economic factors separately misses the strategic importance of the financial sector and how MFCs' entry affects governments.

I propose that a *political-economic* factor, government ownership in the financial sector, explains this variation in fragmented liberalization in finance. I argue that the duality of the government's role in the financial market leads countries to open their financial markets multilaterally for external capital but also embed restrictions to control the speed and extent of liberalization.[5] Furthermore, I argue that the more control a government has over the financial industry, the more entry restrictions it will schedule in its liberalization commitments.

---

[4] Quinn and Inclan 1997.
[5] Many studies have found that state ownership of banks has adverse effects on financial development, private sector development, and the business environment. See Stiglitz 1993; Dinç 2005; Andrianova et al. 2008; Taboada 2011; Grittersová and Mahutga 2020.

72 MAKING FINANCIAL GLOBALIZATION

Governments are important actors in the financial services industry, not only as political bodies but also as market actors. In many countries—democracies and non-democracies, rich and poor—governments have directly or indirectly owned shares in financial firms for strategic reasons. Thus, governments are both *producers* and *users* of financial services, and must balance multiple societal demands as well as their own interests.

Financial liberalization can generate both benefits and costs to governments. The benefits of financial services liberalization include an access to global financial services as well as new capital to domestic firms. Domestic industrial firms, such as those in the agricultural and manufacturing sectors, use financial services to secure loans, insure their products and personnel, and raise capital. However, while liberalization can bring in foreign capital to capital-strapped domestic industrial firms,[6] it can also erode the share of state-owned financial institutions and thus the government's control in the market.[7] More efficient foreign firms may also crowd out inefficient domestic financial firms, including state-owned financial institutions (SOFIs), from the market. Thus, governments face a dilemma between helping industrial firms access global financial services and losing their control of the financial sector.

In order to study the relationship between state ownership in the financial industry and financial trade restrictions, I analyze an original database of financial trade restrictions in 102 countries. I find that the greater a government's control over the financial industry, the more (and more severe) entry restrictions it embeds in its liberalization commitments. My estimates are robust to a set of covariates of the levels of economic, financial, and political development that may affect both the degree of state ownership in finance and the financial entry restrictions. Indeed, the International Monetary Fund (IMF) noted that the "most prominent issues related to the banking sector" in the FSA negotiations were "advocacy for eliminating explicit barriers to foreign entry and urging the sale of government-owned banks."[8]

Once considered a relic of the past, government-owned banks have been quietly resurging around the world. Currently, the world's four largest banks are all owned by the Chinese state: the largest is China's Industrial &

---

[6] Danzman 2019.   [7] Rajan and Zingales 2003; Haber et al. 2008.
[8] IMF Reference Note on Trade in Financial Services, September 3, 2010. Prepared by the Strategy, Policy, and Review and Legal Departments.

Commercial Bank of China (also known as ICBC), followed by China Construction Bank Corp., Agricultural Bank of China, and the Bank of China.[9] China's rise has revived studies of state capitalism in the literature.[10]

In the following section, I explain why the extent of government ownership in the financial industry affects the degree of financial services liberalization. I describe the types of entry barriers and introduce my novel data set on financial trade restrictions. I then quantitatively test how government ownership affects countries' financial trade restrictions.

4.1 Why Does Government Ownership in the Financial Industry Matter?

Government ownership has traditionally been perceived as antithetical to a market economy because the government, rather than the market, would set prices.[11] Developed countries and international organizations have historically championed *laissez-faire* policies and criticized government ownership as competition inhibiting and price distorting. However, state-owned financial institutions have dominated the economies of many developing countries to keep interest rates artificially low and direct credit to emerging industries or national champions.[12] In fact, even some developed countries have had government-owned banks. As discussed in Chapter 1, the French government has traditionally had high levels of ownership in the financial sector.[13] Even the US government, the free market champion, plays an outsized role in the mortgage industry: it sponsors Fannie Mae and Freddie Mac, which finance a large share of all mortgages in the market. In this section, I review *why* governments own financial firms and discuss how this affects their preferences in multilateral liberalization.

Governments own (financial) firms for three strategic and fiscal reasons. First, SOFIs can help governments achieve their political and economic objectives by allocating capital to groups the government considers important to economic growth or political support.[14] For example, while private financial firms may not consider it profitable to invest in infant industries or

---

[9] S&P Global, "The World's 100 Largest Banks 2020."

[10] Baumol et al. 2007; Musacchio et al. 2014.

[11] I thank Judy Goldstein for this point.   [12] Caprio et al. 2010.

[13] The French government has sold off most of its ownership stake in financial firms since the 1970s.

[14] OECD 2018, p. 19.

rural areas due to the inherent risks and large sunk costs,[15] governments can direct capital to such areas through SOFIs. The second reason governments own financial firms is fiscal. SOFIs can bring additional revenues into the state treasury, which can constitute a significant share in developing countries where tax collection is difficult. Some corrupt leaders have even been found to have diverted funds from state-owned enterprises (SOEs) to their personal bank accounts overseas or direct business to firms owned by family or friends.[16] This is why many political leaders directly and indirectly controlled financial firms. In 2018, SOFIs accounted for 40% of assets and 20% of revenues in the financial industry, among the world's 2,000 largest firms.[17] Third, governments around the world have temporarily owned or controlled financial firms during crises to stabilize the financial system (most recently during the 2007–2008 global financial crisis). For example, the US government's capital injection into 707 financial institutions—including top financial firms such as AIG, Citi, Bank of America, and Goldman Sachs— stabilized the country's financial industry during the crisis.

However, government ownership in the financial industry (and economy) generates three main shortcomings. First, it creates a high debt burden. SOFIs, by design, have soft budget constraints. Since many of them do not compete with other firms for survival, they have fewer incentives to be productive and efficient, which leads to high operating costs and low revenues.[18] Moreover, the state's investments in underperforming domestic firms (for political and economic reasons) lead some SOFIs to carry ballooning nonperforming loans (as in the case of Japan in the 1990s and China in the 2000s).

Second, for similar reasons, SOEs fall behind private firms in technological development because they are less likely to invest in updating their technology. This puts them further behind MFCs, which can provide better financial technology and services to their clients. This especially matters for exporters who desire seamless cross-border financial transactions. In a third shortcoming, the dominance of SOEs hampers the emergence of

---

[15] Caprio et al. 2010.

[16] For example, the president of Gambia stole $975 million from the state treasury, including 82% of the revenues of the state-owned telecommunications provider, Gamtel ($364 million). David Pegg, "Gambian Ex-president 'Stole Almost $1bn Before Fleeing Country'," *The Guardian*, March 27, 2019.

[17] International Monetary Fund, *Fiscal Monitor: Policies to Support People During the COVID-19 Pandemic*, Ch 3, "State-Owned Enterprises: The Other Government," p. 49, Figure 3.4. SOEs' Share of Assets, by Sector.

[18] Kornai 1980; Maskin 1996; Budina et al. 1999; Roland 2000.

domestic private enterprises and competition in the industry.[19] Domestic or foreign banks may be dissuaded from entering a market if state-owned banks have firmly established a foothold, given the difficulty of competing with SOFIs. To attract private firms to the market, governments would need to provide assurance to potential entrants that they will be able to operate on a level playing field with SOFIs. These three disadvantages—high debt burden, lagging technological development, and lack of competition—may motivate governments to liberalize and bring in advanced technologies and high-quality services to domestic users.

Governments weigh the costs and benefits of financial liberalization and choose to open up areas in which domestic industrial firms would benefit from MFCs' entry (due to financial linkage) but limit foreign entry in areas that are sensitive to the government, such as retail banking, where SOFIs are dominant. Thus, governments include restrictions while liberalizing to control the pace of foreign entry and protect their SOFIs during the transition.

4.2 Types of Entry Barriers in the Financial Market

Entry barriers allow governments to control whether (and how) foreign firms operate in their markets. Governments can erect a myriad of nontariff entry barriers, which I classify in terms of *what, who, where, when, why,* and *how.* I examine each in detail below, using countries' multilateral liberalization commitments through the FSA.

What. Restrictions on ownership and type of entry are common. When foreign firms enter host markets, they can either establish new enterprises (greenfield investments) or acquire shares of existing firms (mergers and acquisitions). A key business decision relates to ownership, which determines who has management control over a firm: minority (less than 50%), majority (over 50%), or sole (100%) ownership. Foreign firms often face ownership restrictions in host countries due to government fears of losing control of domestic firms to foreign firms that they cannot control.

Ownership restrictions are among the most contentious areas of disagreement between foreign firms and governments. Whole enterprise (100%

---

[19] See Baccini et al. (2019) for the effects of political barriers to entry on SOEs during trade liberalization.

76 MAKING FINANCIAL GLOBALIZATION

ownership) is the most liberal form of entry, and foreign firms' most desired outcome, but it is rare in practice.[20] Some governments' FSA schedules prohibit sole foreign ownership, capping foreign equity participation at less than 50% (minority ownership) or requiring a joint venture (JV) with a local firm (often an SOE) in which management decisions are shared equally.[21] For example, Thailand kept foreign equity participation at under 25%, meaning that locals would have a majority control.[22] Korea limited foreign equity investment in all enterprises to 30% and protected "non-financial conglomerates," known as *chaebols*.[23] China also limited foreign life insurers' business by requiring them to form a JV with a "partner of their choice" at 50% foreign ownership.[24] India went even further to declare that "no income can be received in India from Indian residents."[25] Some countries only allowed MFCs to enter in special economic areas designated for exporters or in offshore areas. For example, Malaysia allowed offshore banking "confined to the Federal Territory of Labuan," an island off its coast.[26]

Who. Some governments also discriminate against foreign firms based on the age and size of the entity; some governments believe large and established enterprises pose fewer risks than small and less established companies. For example, Korea only allowed foreign banks that rank among the world's top 500 "in terms of assets size or representative offices" or those

---

[20] Most foreign firms enter through branches or subsidiaries. The biggest difference between a branch and a subsidiary is where it is incorporated, and thus which regulatory regime it is under. Branches are headquartered in the home country; hence their regulatory jurisdiction is in the home country. Subsidiaries are incorporated in the host country and are therefore subject to host country regulations. Many firms open branches if they want to offer a subset of services, and some firms choose to enter through a subsidiary if they want to engage in a wider and deeper scope of businesses in host markets.

[21] A JV can provide easier access to an established supplier network, an established brand reputation with customers, and favorable financing in the local market. However, a poorly managed JV can result in foreign firms losing technology (and market share) to local firms.

[22] See Thailand's FSA Schedule, GATS/SC/85/Suppl. 3, p. 2.

[23] The Korean government capped equity participation by foreign securities investment trust companies in new or existing JVs with any of the ten largest domestic conglomerates at 30% per foreign company (Korea FSA Schedule, GATS/SC/48/Suppl. 3, p. 12). It also protected its two main SOEs in the primary metal and energy industries: "aggregate foreign investments cannot exceed 23% (18% in the case of two public enterprises: Pohang Iron and Steel Company, Korea Electric Power Corporation) per each company." See Korea's FSA Schedule, GATS/SC/48/Suppl. 3.

[24] China FSA Schedule, GATS/SC/135, p. 29. The Chinese government frequently requires foreign firms to form a JV with a local firm to enter the market. For example, the Shanghai municipal government requires foreign firms to partner with domestic SOEs to facilitate the transfer of technology and management know-how: Volkswagen with its auto SOE, SAIC Motor (Shanghai Automotive Industry Corporation), and Siemens with Shanghai Electric Group for wind turbines.

[25] India FSA Schedule, GATS/SC/42/Suppl. 4.

[26] Malaysia FSA Schedule, GATS/SC/52/Suppl. 3.

that have operated for more than 30 years.[27] Some governments interfere in corporate governance to ensure that firms' managers take national interests into account. Governments want to ensure that at least some MFCs' (and MNCs') profits will be reinvested in the host country. Thus, governments often require that a majority of a firm's board of directors are domestic nationals, hoping they will take national interests into account. For instance, the Philippines required 70% of its banking system's assets to be held by "domestic banks which are at least majority-owned by Filipinos,"[28] and Thailand required a three-quarters majority for finance companies.[29] The United States required board members of foreign financial firms to be US citizens; in Louisiana, 100% of the board members of locally established and licensed companies were required to be US citizens, two-thirds in Pennsylvania, and a majority in Indiana, Kentucky, and New York.[30] Some countries extended the citizenship requirement to the nonmanagement level. For example, Thailand limited the number of foreign personnel to two for a representative office and six for each fully licensed branch.[31]

Where. Some governments limit foreign firms' geographic scope to restrict foreign exposure to a limited area and protect domestic firms. Financial linkage can often predict where foreign enterprises will be allowed to operate, such as industrial centers or special economic zones, where domestic and foreign enterprises can benefit from accessing foreign financial services. For example, China initially allowed foreign insurers in only five special economic zones (Shanghai, Guangzhou, Dalian, Shenzhen, and Foshan). Within two years after its accession to the WTO, China opened up 10 more cities, including Beijing and nearby Tianjin, before removing geographic restrictions.[32]

When. To give domestic financial firms time to adjust to liberalization, governments also restrict the timing of entry in two ways: grandfathering the rights of foreign firms that have already entered (standstill) or promising to open later (future promises). Many foreign firms oppose the former, as it is more restrictive. For example, Thailand only allows foreign financial

---

[27] Korea FSA Schedule, GATS/SC/48/Suppl. 3, p. 7.
[28] Philippines FSA Schedule, GATS/SC/70/Suppl. 3, p. 2.
[29] Thailand FSA Schedule, GATS/SC/85/Suppl. 3, p. 12.
[30] US FSA Schedule, GATS/SC/90/Suppl. 3, p. 5.
[31] Thailand FSA Schedule, GATS/SC/85/Suppl. 3, p. 14.
[32] The other eight are Chengdu, Chongqing, Fuzhou, Ningbo, Shenyang, Suzhou, Wuhan, and Xiamen.

firms to acquire shares in existing companies.[33] An example of the latter is the Chinese government's promise to allow wholly foreign-owned subsidiaries within five years of its accession in 2002.[34]

How. Governments can restrict the entry of foreign firms by class or on a case-by-case basis. Class restrictions apply to all firms that belong to a certain category, such as all non-life-insurance firms, regardless of individual firm characteristics. Governments can also restrict entry on a case-by-case basis, even in the same class of business. A common restriction in this category is mandating presidential or congressional approval for each entry case. For example, Brazil subjects foreign financial firms' entry requests to a "case-by-case authorization by the Executive Branch, by means of a Presidential decree."[35] Thailand similarly requires a "license approved by the Minister with the consent of the Cabinet," which is quite restrictive to get an approval from the Cabinet for each entry application.[36] Case-by-case restrictions are more discriminatory because they are applied on an ad hoc basis, which increases foreign firms' uncertainty and search costs but offers governments flexibility.

Why. Governments can require foreign entrants to justify how they would benefit the local economy, also known as an "economic needs test." For example, the Philippines included a restriction requiring the regulator to "determine whether public interest and economic conditions justify authorization for the establishment of commercial presence or expansion of existing operations in banking and other financial services in the Philippines." MFCs must demonstrate they can "contribute to the attainment of Philippine development objectives particularly in the promotion of trade, investments and appropriate technology transfer"; this is also quite restrictive for financial firms to justify their entry.[37]

These six types of restrictions—what, who, when, where, how, and why—demonstrate the extent to which governments restrict foreign entry during liberalization. In the next section I describe a new database that quantifies these entry restrictions in trade in financial services in 102 countries.

---

[33] Thailand FSA Schedule, GATS/SC/85/Suppl. 3, p. 11.
[34] China's FSA Schedule, GATS/SC/135.
[35] Brazil FSA Schedule, GATS/SC/13/Suppl. 3, p. 5.
[36] GATS/SC/85/Suppl. 3, p. 2.   [37] GATS/SC/70/Suppl. 3, p. 2.

4.3 Analysis: Government Ownership and Financial Trade Liberalization

In this section, I examine the statistical relationship between government ownership and countries' degree of liberalization in the financial industry. The analysis is necessarily cross-sectional, because the restrictions created by the multilateral agreement in trade in financial services are essentially constant over time.[38] First, I describe a new database of financial trade restrictions, which coded the final FSA commitment schedules for all 102 signatories submitted between the interim round in 1994 and the final round in 1997.[39] A financial liberalization schedule contains an $m*n$ matrix, in which m is the type of financial service business, which is broadly divided into two categories—insurance services and banking and other noninsurance financial services—and n denotes the type of restriction, such as ownership and minimum capital requirements.[40] The insurance subsector is divided into five subcategories: life insurance, non-life insurance, reinsurance, insurance intermediation (such as agency and brokerage), and auxiliary insurance services (e.g., actuarial services or insurance and pension consultancy services). The banking subsector is divided into two subcategories: banking and nonbanking financial services. Banking services include acceptance of deposits, lending of all types (including mortgages, credit cards, etc.), financial leasing, guarantees and commitments, and payment and money transmission services. Nonbanking financial services include trading, securities issuance (including securities underwriting), money brokerage, asset management, financial consultancy, and financial information provision.

Figure 4.2 is an example of the US liberalization schedule. It displays the restrictions in direct insurance (life, accident, health insurance, and non-life-insurance services). It shows that the US has market access restrictions that prohibit foreign government-owned or government-controlled insurance

---

[38] The EU and Brazil updated once in 2019 after 22 years, and their restrictions changed little.

[39] If countries updated their 1994 schedules, I replaced the old schedules with their updated schedules in 1997.

[40] Financial services schedules follow the positive-list style of the General Agreement on Trade in Services (GATS); countries specify the (sub)sectors to be liberalized. Negative-list styles only exclude the listed (sub)sectors from liberalization. Schedules list horizontal restrictions that apply to the financial sector in general as well as specific restrictions that apply to subsectors of financial services.

Modes of supply: 1) Cross-border supply 2) Consumption abroad 3) Commercial presence 4) Presence of natural persons

Sector or Sub-sector	Limitations on Market Access	Limitations on National Treatment	Additional Commitments
7. FINANCIAL SERVICES **A. INSURANCE:**			
1. Commitments in this subsector are undertaken in accordance with the Understanding on Commitments in Financial Services (the "Understanding"), subject to the limitations and conditions set forth in these headnotes and the schedule below.			
2. The market access commitments in this subsector in respect of mode (1), as described in paragraph 2(a) of Article I of the Agreement, are limited to the services indicated in paragraphs B.3(a) and B.3(b) of the market access section of the Understanding. The market access commitments in this subsector in respect of mode (2), as described in paragraph 2(b) of Article I of the Agreement, are limited to the services indicated in paragraphs B.4(a) and B.4(b) of the market access section of the Understanding. It is understood that paragraph B.4 of the Understanding does not require that non-resident financial service suppliers be permitted to solicit business, and no commitment to such solicitation is undertaken.			
3. National treatment commitments in this subsector are subject to the following limitation: national treatment with respect to services and service suppliers will be provided according to a non-U.S. service supplier's state of domicile, where applicable, in the United States. State of domicile is defined by individual states, and is generally the state in which an insurer either is incorporated, is organized or maintains its principal office in the United States.			
4. Commitments in this sector do not cover measures set out in the entry applicable to "Insurance" in the United States list of exemptions from Article II.			
Direct Insurance a) Life, Accident, and Health Insurance Services (except workers compensation insurance) b) Non-Life Insurance Services	1) Government-owned or government-controlled insurance companies, whether US or foreign, are not authorized to conduct business in: Alabama, Alaska, Arkansas, California, Colorado, Connecticut, Delaware, Georgia, Hawaii, Idaho, Kansas, Kentucky, Maine, Maryland, Montana, Nevada, New Jersey (only with respect to surplus lines), New York (non-life companies are authorized; life and health companies are not), North Carolina, North Dakota, Oklahoma, Oregon, Pennsylvania, Rhode Island, South Dakota, Tennessee, Washington, West Virginia, Wyoming.	1) A one per cent federal excise tax is imposed on all life insurance premiums and a four per cent federal excise tax is imposed on all non-life insurance premiums covering US risks that are paid to companies not incorporated under US law, except for premiums that are earned by such companies through an office or dependent agent in the United States. When more than 50 per cent of the value of a maritime vessel whose hull was built under federally guaranteed mortgage funds is insured by a non-US insurer, the insured must demonstrate that the risk was substantially first offered in the US market.	The United States undertakes the obligations contained in Additional Commitments Paper I attached hereto.

Figure 4.2 Excerpt of the US FSA schedule. This page details US general commitments in the insurance sector (7. Financial Services A. Insurance) as well as specific commitments within the insurance sector such as direct insurance (life, accident, health insurance services, and non-life-insurance services). The schedule has two main types of restrictions on market access (second column) and national treatment (third column). The FSA schedule also denotes the modes of supply with numbers: (1) cross-border supply, (2) consumption abroad, (3) commercial presence, and (4) presence of natural persons. To calculate the number of restrictions, I sum the restrictions across all modes of supply (1–4). To assess their severity, I code each mode separately, focusing on Mode 3, the most contentious; I also analyze other modes of supply.

companies from conducting business in 29 US states, from Alabama to Wyoming.[41]

There are two ways to measure a country's level of financial openness: the number of entry restrictions in the financial industry and their severity. The following two sections discuss each in turn.

4.3.1 Number of Restrictions

I create a measure of market access limitations listed in each country's WTO liberalization schedule by the mode of supply. For each subcategory of financial services, I assign a value of 1 if there is at least one restriction for that mode and 0 otherwise. For example, if life insurance services have a restriction in Mode 3, I assign 1 for that mode. A country with one restriction in Mode 1, no restrictions in Mode 2, three restrictions in Mode 3, and closed to entry (unbound) in Mode 4 for life insurance would be coded 1, 0, 1, 1. Thus, the number of restrictions in the life insurance business would be 4 for that country. To create my final measure, I sum all subcategories across the four modes of service for each country. Thus, my measure captures the extent of government control of foreign entry in specific business areas (i.e., life insurance, non-life insurance, reinsurance, banking, securities).

4.3.2 Severity-Weighted Entry Restrictions

Whether a country has a number of restrictions may be different from how severe those restrictions are. Thus, I also measure the severity of restrictions across the four modes of supply, from 0 (open) to 3 (closed).[42] In each type of restriction, I coded four categories, from least to most severe: (i) none, (ii) class-based restrictions, (iii) case-by-case approval, and (iv) unbound (no liberalization). The theoretical upper bound of this measure is the

---

[41] Liberalization restrictions are largely divided into two types of limitations: market access and national treatment. The former refers to entry barriers for foreign financial services providers, while the latter denotes discriminatory treatment between domestic and foreign providers. Each type of limitation contains restrictions based on four modes of supply. This chapter focuses on market access limitations in order to analyze entry barriers.

[42] I further divide commercial presence (Mode 3), which deals directly with foreign direct investment (FDI) in host countries. This mode comprises of three types of restrictions: ownership, entry, and nationality of personnel.

unboundedness of the (sub)sector, in which a sector is closed to foreign entry (no liberalization). Class-based restrictions include restrictions on the types of businesses allowed (life insurance allowed but reinsurance not allowed, etc.), types of entry (branches allowed but subsidiaries not allowed, etc.), and geographic locations (only opening to specific cities). Case-by-case restrictions include economic needs tests, prudential criteria, capital control, and prohibiting business with locals. These are more restrictive than class-based restrictions that are applied to a whole set of businesses. An example of a severity-weighted entry restrictions coding is as follows: if a country allows 100% ownership in life insurance for Mode 1 and 49% ownership in depository banking for Mode 3, it would receive a rating of 1 for the first restriction and 3 (more severe) for the second.

4.3.3 Distribution of Entry Restrictions

Figure 4.3 illustrates the distribution of entry restrictions in 102 countries. These restrictions are distributed with a long right tail, meaning that roughly half of the sample has few restrictions. The left panel illustrates the distribution of the *number* of restrictions. Nearly half of the countries in the

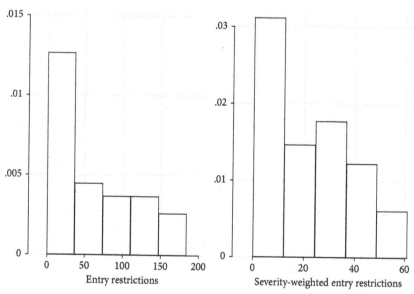

Figure 4.3 Distribution of entry restrictions. The left panel displays the distribution of entry restrictions, and the right panel illustrates the distribution of severity-weighted entry restrictions. About 30–40% of countries are in the lowest bin, and most of them have nonzero values.

FRAGMENTED LIBERALIZATION IN THE FINANCIAL INDUSTRY 83

sample have 0–20 restrictions (very few have none, but many have a few restrictions); the other half is divided between the medium (21–40) and high groups (41–63), with a mean of 25 and a median of 21. The distribution of the number of financial restrictions ranges from 0 in Barbados and 1 in Trinidad and Tobago to 61 in Brazil and 63 in South Africa. The low-restriction group includes countries with varying GDP levels, from France and Germany to Colombia, Qatar, and Zimbabwe.

Interestingly, in contrast to the patterns expected by the theory of comparative advantages, which would expect that countries with comparative advantages in financial services would be more open than those without, least developed countries did not schedule many restrictions, either because they wanted to attract financial services from abroad or because many of them, especially former colonies, already had a large foreign banking presence. The medium group includes a variety of countries, such as Argentina, Bahrain, Indonesia, Kenya, and the US. The high-restriction group includes emerging markets in middle- to high-income countries, such as Brazil, China, Israel, Korea, and Singapore.

The right panel displays the distribution of the *severity* of the entry restrictions. Cuba, Denmark, Greece, and Malawi have less severe restrictions, while those in the most severe restriction group include Canada, Korea, the Philippines, and Thailand. Both graphs exhibit a similar structure: about half of the countries in the sample have 0–20 restrictions.

4.3.4 Model and Data

For the empirical modeling strategy, I use a median regression model (Koenker and Hallock 2001) due to the heavily skewed nature of the dependent variable. To measure my central explanatory variable, *government ownership in the financial industry*, I use the share of government ownership data from La Porta et al. (2002), which measures the share of the assets of a country's top 10 banks owned by the government, scaled between 0 and 1. This data is available for 92 countries.

Economic variables. I include economic variables that could affect both government ownership of the financial industry and the level of entry restrictions, including GDP per capita, the level of exports, FDI inflows, and import of trade in financial services.[43] Since rich countries may be more

---

[43] Data for GDP per capita, population size, and export level comes from the World Bank's World Development Indicator. The data on the import of trade in financial and insurance services comes from UNCTAD.

84 MAKING FINANCIAL GLOBALIZATION

likely to liberalize their financial industry than poor ones, I use GDP per capita (log) to account for levels of economic development. Similarly, if a country is an active exporter, it may have fewer and less severe restrictions in the financial services sector in order to help its domestic exporters. Countries that receive large FDI inflows may also have fewer and less severe restrictions to attract more capital. Thus, my models include variables for FDI inflows (log) and trade in financial services imports. Countries that import a large amount of financial services either have fewer and less severe restrictions if they would like to continue importing, or increase their number and severity if they would like to restrict their already high levels of imports.

Political variables. Political confounders include regime type, property rights, and corruption. Several prior studies have found that democracies attract trade and investment. I therefore use the standard Polity IV score to indicate the level of democracy (-10 = least democratic; $+10$ = most democratic).[44] The model also controls for property rights: if a country has strong property rights, governments would not need to restrict foreign firms from entering, since it has a strong rule of law to adjudicate potential disputes after entry.[45] I expect countries with strong property rights to have fewer restrictions. Finally, corruption may capture residual political problems in host countries that may affect their level of financial liberalization. In a highly corrupt society, especially if government leaders and their families control the SOEs, foreign firms may face entry barriers and discrimination in those markets.[46] For all these variables, I use cross-sectional averages 10 years prior to the treaty's signing.

Table 4.1 reports coefficient estimates from a robust regression model with heteroskedastic standard errors. In Model 1, a one-unit increase in government ownership of financial firms yields an estimated increase of 74.17 restrictions; this estimate is not statistically different from zero (at the 5% significance level used throughout the study). However, when economic characteristics are added in Model 2, a one-standard-deviation increase in state ownership increases the number of restrictions by 52.88. After accounting for both economic and political characteristics (including controls for GDP per capita, population, exports, FDI inflows per GDP, foreign bank share, Polity score, and property rights), a one-standard-deviation increase

---

[44] Data comes from the Polity IV database.
[45] The data on property rights comes from La Porta et al. 2002.
[46] I use the data from La Porta et al. 2002.

Table 4.1 Regression of Number of Restrictions and Severity-Weighted Restrictions on Government Ownership

	Number of Restrictions				Severity-Weighted	
	(1)	(2)	(3)	(4)	(5)	(6)
Govt. Ownership	74.172	52.878*	65.924*	68.723*	19.928*	20.208*
	(41.673)	(22.711)	(23.507)	(25.531)	(5.856)	(8.388)
GDP per capita		−79.459*	−84.786*	−89.608*	−26.835*	−28.107*
		(14.212)	(15.925)	(17.051)	(4.414)	(6.464)
Total Population		−40.457*	−43.929*	−46.955*	−13.097*	−13.892*
		(13.138)	(12.576)	(13.491)	(3.425)	(4.277)
Exports		38.650*	35.180*	39.412*	11.249*	10.777*
		(9.074)	(11.055)	(11.576)	(3.733)	(5.010)
FDI Inflows		16.300	20.578*	19.767	5.678*	6.841*
		(9.347)	(8.577)	(10.330)	(2.465)	(3.296)
Foreign Bank Share		0.011	0.153	−0.063	−0.013	−0.101
		(0.346)	(0.338)	(0.349)	(0.132)	(0.139)
Polity			1.013	0.937	−0.158	−0.033
			(1.700)	(2.248)	(0.577)	(0.730)
Property Rights			5.038	10.306	2.605	5.701
			(8.850)	(12.013)	(2.852)	(4.374)
Corruption				−0.841		−0.831
				(5.387)		(2.009)
Observations	75	64	62	60	67	62

Robust Standard Errors in parentheses.

$^{*}\ p < 0.05$

in state ownership increases the number of restrictions by 65.92 in Model 3. Model 4 adds controls for corruption that capture other residual factors that affect restrictions on foreign entry. Even after adding the corruption measure, government ownership remains similar at an increase of 68.72 FDI restrictions.

In addition to the width of restrictions, I also examine their *depth*. I test how government ownership affects the severity of restrictions by weighting each restriction according to its level of severity. Some countries may have many restrictions, but some of them may be less severe. Models 5 and 6 establish that government ownership of banks leads to a statistically significant increase of 20 severity-weighted restrictions. The coefficients are smaller because the severity-weighted restrictions range from 0 to 61 instead of 0 to 180, as shown in Figure 4.3. Government ownership increases both the number and severity of financial FDI restrictions. Governments embed more restrictions while liberalizing to control the speed and extent

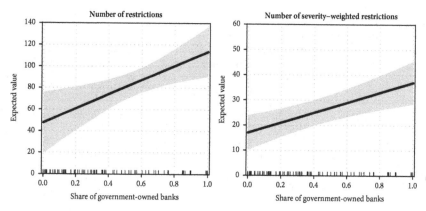

Figure 4.4 Effect of government ownership on entry barriers in finance.

of liberalization, and thereby maintain their influence over the financial market.

Figure 4.4 plots the expected values of entry barriers, with 95% confidence intervals given the share of government ownership of banks, keeping the control variables at their observed values. The left panel displays the expected number of restrictions, and the right panel displays the expected number of *severity-weighted* restrictions. The sample distribution of government-owned banks, from 0 (no government ownership) to 1 (full government ownership), is depicted as a rug plot at the bottom of the figure. This figure indicates that as government ownership of banks increases, the median number of entry restrictions also increases.

When the share of government-owned banks increases from 0 to 0.8, the median number of entry barriers rises from 50 to 90, which represents an increase from the level of Turkey and Ghana (50) to that of the Dominican Republic (89) and Argentina (92). As government ownership surges from the median to the 75th percentile, the expected number of restrictions rises by 17—equivalent to moving from Malta's level of liberalization to that of Romania. Increasing a country's government ownership level from the 25th to the 95th percentile predicts an increase in the expected number of restrictions of 53, which is roughly equivalent to a rise from Kenya's level of liberalization to that of Kuwait. The right panel displays a similar relationship: as government ownership of banks increases, the median number of severity-weighted restrictions increases.

FRAGMENTED LIBERALIZATION IN THE FINANCIAL INDUSTRY

Table 4.2 Robustness Checks

	Estimate	SE	N
(1) Financial development	49.967	(19.436)	64
(2) Asian financial crisis	52.878	(25.286)	61
(3) World region FE	69.066	(19.362)	64

Note: Based on Specification (3) in Table 4.1. Robust standard errors in parentheses.

4.3.5 Robustness Tests

Since other factors could boost government ownership of financial firms as well as the number and severity of financial trade restrictions, I subject my results to three further robustness tests (results displayed in Table 4.2).

(1) Level of financial development. A developed financial market may have fewer restrictions than an underdeveloped one. Accounting for the level of financial development, the effects of government-owned banks are still significant at around 50 restrictions.

(2) Asian financial crisis. I test to see if the crisis, which occurred during the negotiations, affected countries' entry restrictions. I control for the countries that were directly affected and received IMF loans, such as Korea, Indonesia, and Thailand, as well as those that were indirectly affected by the crisis, such as Hong Kong, Malaysia, and the Philippines. The results for government ownership stay the same—an increase of around 53 restrictions at the 99.9% level of statistical significance.

(3) Region fixed effects. I include region fixed effects (Asia, Europe, Americas, Africa, and Oceania) to control for region-specific differences. The results remain approximately the same at 69 restrictions.

4.4 Conclusion

In this chapter I examined why governments agreed to liberalize financial services through a multilateral agreement but included restrictions in their commitments. While the conventional wisdom would expect political regime type or economic size to explain liberalization, I argue that

88 MAKING FINANCIAL GLOBALIZATION

governments' control of financial institutions, either through SOFIs or domestic financial firms, leads them to include restrictions while liberalizing to protect their control over the financial industry. Since governments represent not only societal interests but also their own interests in the financial market, they liberalized their financial markets to reap the benefits of financial linkage but still included restrictions to control the pace and extent of foreign entry into their financial markets.

Using a new database on financial entry restrictions, this chapter showed that indeed governments with a higher share of ownership in financial firms included more restrictions in their liberalization schedules. This relationship holds across different levels of economic development, and regime types. While some governments set their restrictions to expire after a short adjustment period, others kept them until they reformed their domestic regulations and/or signed free trade agreements with other countries. Brazil, for example, maintained most of its restrictions until 2019, when it submitted an updated schedule.

This chapter showed that while an international agreement was created to facilitate international banks' expansion to financial markets around the world, governments still included restrictions while liberalizing. These restrictions were more severe in areas over which governments had more control. Governments have a direct interest in protecting their market share and control while promoting economic growth and helping industrial firms, especially those engaged in international trade. Examining a government's multidimensional preferences in the financial industry contributes to the literature by moving beyond the dichotomy of liberalization and protection to explain the nuanced way in which governments embed restrictions while liberalizing to maximize gains while minimizing the costs.

5

De Jure Liberalization

Lowering Entry Regulations

The theoretical framework of multilateral lobbying described how multinational financial corporations (MFCs), which faced various entry regulations in their international expansion, sought to create an international liberalization framework that could produce concurrent domestic regulatory changes. To determine if their lobbying efforts were successful, this chapter investigates whether countries around the world changed their financial entry regulations in line with the principles of the World Trade Organization (WTO) Financial Services Agreement (FSA), such as those related to independent regulation, market access, and nondiscrimination.

Many previous studies have explored how international agreements affect states' behaviors, but the findings have been mixed.[1] Some found that international agreements led to changes in states' behavior, while others identified null or even negative effects.[2] One of the most challenging problems associated with identifying the effects of international agreements is the selection problem: such agreements reflect states' preferences, so the agreed state behavior would have occurred even without the agreement.[3] In this case, countries that joined the FSA would have changed their domestic regulations even without the agreement. In international relations, it is difficult to investigate the counterfactual—what countries would have done had they not signed the agreement (in the potential outcome framework). This is an especially acute problem of inference in international negotiations, since it is not exogenous to states' behaviors. Countries actively participate in international negotiations to create an agreement. Thus, I cannot identify the causal effect of international agreements on domestic regulatory reforms.

---

[1] For studies on the effectiveness of international agreements on human rights, trade, monetary affairs, and the environment, see Keohane 1984; Hathaway 2007; Goldstein et al. 2007; Tomz et al. 2007; Simmons 2000; Kerner 2009.

[2] Downs et al. 1996; Wirth 1997; Rose 2004; Von Stein 2005; Hathaway 2007.

[3] Von Stein 2005.

Making Financial Globalization: How Firms Shape International Regulatory Cooperation. Clara Park, Oxford University Press. © Oxford University Press 2025. DOI: 10.1093/oso/9780197761816.003.0005

90 MAKING FINANCIAL GLOBALIZATION

Instead, I examine whether the FSA served as *focal point* on which countries converged their domestic financial regulatory reforms to an agreed set of norms. The FSA created a new international regime in trade in financial services liberalization and laid out specific norms, principles, rules, and procedures on independent regulation and liberalization, especially related to ownership, market access, and nondiscrimination. I examine whether countries implemented domestic regulatory reforms that lowered their entry barriers and created independent financial regulators in line with these FSA norms and procedures. This approach can show whether the international agreement influenced countries' regulatory harmonization to a set of agreed-upon liberalization norms and independent regulation among all available choices in domestic financial reforms.

I created a database of financial regulations before and after the FSA negotiations for 148 countries. I found that the FSA did serve as a focal point around which countries harmonized their financial regulatory changes, resulting in *de jure* liberalization. The agreement led to changes in domestic regulations and weakened restrictions against foreign entry in the financial industry all over the world. The FSA helped reduce transaction costs and spread norms of liberalization, market access, and independent regulation, all of which led to changes in domestic regulations. Many countries also created independent financial regulators.

I discuss two mechanisms through which the FSA shaped financial regulatory reforms around the world: a new international regime (norms, principles, rules, and procedures) and a depository of financial regulations. Next, I analyze whether countries have changed their domestic regulations in line with the FSA commitments in Latin America and East Asia, key markets of interest to MFCs. I then present a case study of the domestic regulatory changes in the US and China following their multilateral FSA commitments.

5.1 Mechanisms

I advance two mechanisms through which an international agreement generated domestic regulatory changes. The first was a new international regime that laid out specific norms, principles, rules, and procedures in trade in financial services—such as independent regulator, nondiscrimination, and transparency—that countries incorporated into their domestic regulatory reforms. The second mechanism entailed creating an international depository of past, present, and future regulations, which reduces information asymmetry for foreign entrants and facilitates MFCs' international expansion. The remainder of the section examines these mechanisms in more detail.

5.1.1 Creating a New International Regime

The FSA created a new international regime of open, transparent, and nondiscriminatory regulations that helped financial firms expand abroad and operate on a more level playing field with domestic firms. The FSA promoted two key WTO principles: (1) most-favored nation (MFN) status (extending privileges granted to one trading partner to all signatories) and (2) national treatment (treating domestic and foreign firms the same; i.e., without discriminating against foreign firms).[4] Under these broad categories, the FSA specifically pushed for norms on independent regulation, monopolies, new financial services, and financial information transmission. I describe each category below.

The first type of norm that countries strongly pushed through the FSA was *independent regulation*. Many countries' financial regulators were previously not independent from state-owned financial institutions (SOFIs). This created problems for foreign entrants because the regulator also operated their competitors, SOFIs, in host markets. An independent regulator would reduce such conflicts of interest. Thus, the FSA pushed countries to create independent financial regulators to ensure a level playing field between foreign entrants and domestic financial firms, including SOFIs.

Second, the FSA tried to reduce the scope of state-protected financial *monopolies*. Some countries excluded their monopolies from multilateral liberalization in the FSA schedules, such as motor vehicle insurance (i.e., Canada),[5] reinsurance (i.e., Cambodia),[6] fire and natural damage insurance (Switzerland), and postal administration (Finland and Cote d'Ivoire). Though the FSA acknowledged each signatory's right to protect its "existing monopoly rights," it also encouraged countries to "endeavour to eliminate

---

[4] The FSA establishes norms through two multilateral frameworks: The Understanding on Commitments in Financial Services and the Annex on Financial Services.

[5] Other countries include the Czech Republic and Slovakia.

[6] Other countries include the Philippines, Kenya, Nigeria, Senegal, Turkey, and Morocco.

92 MAKING FINANCIAL GLOBALIZATION

them or reduce their scope" in the future to liberalize entry into their financial markets.[7]

Third, the FSA asked governments to allow financial service providers to offer *new financial services*.[8] Many signatories, especially developing countries, were hesitant to allow new complex financial products in their markets due to their lack of regulatory expertise in the financial market. This created problems for MFCs, which wanted to offer new products beyond basic financial services in host markets. Thus, MFCs lobbied government negotiators to allow new services through the FSA.

Fourth, the agreement pressured governments to allow the *cross-border transfer of financial data*.[9] MFCs want to transfer users' data to their data centers across borders for processing and sale of data, while many governments seek to protect the privacy and security of their citizens' information and keep data within their borders. Since commercial interests conflict with security and privacy interests, cross-border data transfer has been a thorny issue in many countries. The FSA acknowledged governments' desire to protect citizens' data but asked them to allow the cross-border transfer of financial information as long as it does not "circumvent the provisions of the Agreement."[10] This "data localization" problem is not unique to financial services; it remains one of the most hotly debated issues in technology.

While the FSA created a new regime in financial services liberalization, it also included two important limitations on liberalization. First, the agreement excluded "services supplied in the exercise of governmental authority," such as monetary or exchange rate policies and social security or public retirement plans.[11] During the FSA negotiations, finance ministers were concerned that the FSA would hinder governments' monetary and social policies. Thus, the FSA explicitly excluded non-entry-related government policies to placate financial ministers.

---

[7] Understanding on Commitments in Financial Services, B.1.

[8] "A member shall permit financial service suppliers of any other Member established in its territory to offer in its territory any new financial service" (Understanding on Commitments in Financial Services, B., New Financial Services 7).

[9] "No member shall take measures that prevent transfers of information or the processing of financial information, including transfers of data by electronic means" (Understanding on Commitments in Financial Services, B., Transfers of Information and Processing Information 8).

[10] "Nothing in this paragraph restricts the right of a Member to protect personal data, personal privacy and the confidentiality of individual records and accounts so long as such right is not used to circumvent the provisions of the Agreement" (Understanding on Commitments in Financial Services, B., Transfers of Information and Processing Information 8).

[11] Kireyev 2002.

In a second important limitation on liberalization, the FSA preserved governments' ability to escape from compliance in times of crisis.[12] Developing countries were especially concerned that a multilateral liberalization agreement would tie their hands and limit their ability to respond to financial crises. The Asian financial crisis and capital flight that occurred during the FSA negotiations amplified this fear. Thus, the FSA included flexibility provisions that allowed countries to suspend compliance for "prudential reasons" such as protecting investors or depositors to "ensure the integrity and stability of the financial system."[13] These provisions were tested 10 years later during the 2007 global financial crisis, when *developed* countries such as the US temporarily suspended their FSA commitments to inject public capital and bail out their banks.[14]

5.1.2 Creating an International Depository of Financial Regulations

The second mechanism via which the FSA encouraged domestic regulatory changes was creating an international depository of financial regulations. For decades, many countries lacked clear rules of foreign entry and granted access to their markets on a case-by-case basis. This process was so fraught with uncertainty and information asymmetry that entrants had to hire international and domestic lawyers, consultants, and sometimes power brokers or politicians' family to navigate them.[15] The central depository of regulations facilitates information transfers and enhances transparency.

To reduce uncertainty and the transaction costs of entry negotiations, the FSA created an international depository of financial regulations in

---

[12] Rosendorff and Milner 2001.

[13] "A Member shall not be prevented from taking measures for prudential reasons, including for the protection of investors, depositors, policy holders or persons to whom a fiduciary duty is owned by a financial service supplier, or to ensure the integrity and stability of the financial system. Where such measures do not conform with the provisions of the Agreement, they shall not be used as a means of avoiding the Member's commitments or obligations under the Agreement. Nothing in the Agreement shall be construed to require a Member to disclose information relating to the affairs and accounts of individual customers or any confidential or proprietary information in the possession of public entities" (GATS Annex on Financial Services, 2. Domestic Regulation).

[14] Some foreign counterparts, such as Barbados and Ecuador, criticized the bailouts as discriminating against foreign banks. See Gretchen Morgenson, "Barriers to Change, From Wall St. and Geneva," *New York Times*, March 17, 2012.

[15] David Lynch, Jennifer Hughes, and Martin Arnold, "JPMorgan To Pay $264m Penalty for Hiring 'Princelings,'" *Financial Times*, November 17, 2016.

94 MAKING FINANCIAL GLOBALIZATION

which countries listed their past, present, and future regulatory reforms to lower entry barriers and create independent financial regulators in their FSA commitments. Tables 5.1 and 5.2 list countries' domestic regulations relevant to trade in financial services in their FSA liberalization schedules. Almost half (46%) of the signatories specified at least one existing domestic regulation that governed foreign entry and operation in the financial market, and 19% listed at least two regulations. These regulations included laws on finance (i.e., Jamaica, Kenya), insurance (i.e., Brazil, Cote d'Ivoire, Cyprus), and securities (i.e., Korea), as well as laws that established central banks. These legislations govern foreign entry into their financial markets through licensing requirements, such as ownership restrictions, minimum capital requirements, and branches and subsidiary requirements.

Some countries also included discussions of their forthcoming financial regulations in their FSA schedules. For example, the US stated that the Federal Reserve, along with other domestic regulators, had "established an enhanced framework for the regulation and supervision of U.S. operations of foreign banks."[16] Brazil promised foreign entry into the reinsurance market pending regulatory changes. Four Eastern European countries listed ongoing regulatory reforms in their FSA schedules, including reforms on market access (Czech Republic and Hungary), prudential regulations (Poland), and a Law on Banking (Slovenia).[17]

The FSA also contained regulations not directly related to the financial industry but which would affect foreign entry and operation in financial services, such as competition, tax, labor, and land laws. Upon entry, foreign firms employ local citizens and buy land for their offices in host markets, which are subject to local regulations. Thus, some countries listed laws regarding foreign entry in their FSA schedules, such as income tax law (Canada, Dominica), labor code (Guatemala), and alien land law (China, Korea, and the Caribbean Islands). Moreover, because finance covers

---

[16] US FSA schedule, GATS/SC/90/Suppl. 3, p. 31.

[17] Czech Republic noted in its FSA schedule, "Legislation covering the abolition of the criterion of financial market requirements is now being discussed in the Parliament" (GATS/SC/26/Suppl. 3, p. 8). Hungary noted, "Legislation permitting market access of branches is currently being prepared" (GATS/SC/40/Suppl. 3, p. 2). Poland specified that it was creating prudential regulations in accordance with the FSA commitments in its schedule: "Prudential regulations in the financial sector are being elaborated in Poland.... Their application will be done in accordance with the provisions of the Annex on Financial Services, paragraph 2 - Domestic Regulation sub-paragraph 1" (GATS/SC/71/Suppl. 3, p. 2). Slovenia mentioned two regulatory developments in finance at the time of the FSA negotiations, including the adoption of a new Law on Banking (GATS/SC/99/Suppl. 1, p. 12).

DE JURE LIBERALIZATION   95

Table 5.1 Domestic Finance Legislation Listed in Countries' FSA Schedules

Country	Legislation
Angola	Decree 16/94 of April 22, 1994 of the Council of Ministers
Australia	Trust Bank (Corporation) Act 1997
Austria	Community Law
Bahrain	Bahrain Monetary Agency Law (Amiri Decree - Law No. (23) of 1973
Benin	Law No. 90-018 of July 27, 1990
Bolivia	National Law
Brazil	Brazilian reinsurance institution (IRB-Brasil Resseguros S.A.)
Bulgaria	Trade Law
Canada	Income Tax Act of Canada
Chile	Law No. 18840 (Central Bank of Chile)
Cyprus	Insurance Companies Law
Czech Republic	Insurance Industry Act
Dominica	Witholding Tax Provisions of the Income Tax Act
Ecuador	General Law on Insurance Companies
Egypt	Law No. 37 of 1992, Article 13
Estonia	Registration under Estonian Law as a joint stock company, subsidiary, or branch
EU	UCITS Directive, 85/611/EEC, Articles 6 and 13
Grenada	Exchange Control Act
Guatemala	Labor Code
Israel	Currency Control Law, 6738-1978
Italy	Article 18 of Law 216/74
Ivory Coast	Insurance Code of the Inter-African Conference on Insurance Markets (CIMA)
Jamaica	Banking Act (Part III, Section 6:1(a) on Capital and Reserves)
Kenya	Banking Act
Korea	Securities Exchange Act
Lesotho	Companies Act
Lichtenstein	Lichtenstein Banking and Financial Companies Act
Macau	Financial System Act of Macau
Mauritius	Road Traffic Act 1963 (compulsory third-party insurance)
Morocco	Exchange regulations
Mozambique	Domestic rules and regulations
New Zealand	Financial Reporting Act 1993
Nicaragua	General Law on Insurance Institutions
Nigeria	Investment Promotion Commission Decree of 1995
Pakistan	Foreign exchange laws
Poland	Requirement to use the public telecommunications network
Romania	(Civil) Romanian law
Saudi Arabia	Companies Act
Senegal	Insurance Code of the Inter-African Insurance Market Conference (CIMA)

commodity trading, some countries included regulations on agricultural commodities, such as the Onion Futures Act (US) and the Apple and Pear Marketing Act and Wheat Producers Levy Act (New Zealand).

96 MAKING FINANCIAL GLOBALIZATION

Table 5.2 Domestic Finance Legislation Listed in Countries' FSA Schedules, Continued

Country	Legislation
Slovak Republic	Banking Act
Slovenia	Law on Commercial Companies
Taiwan	Futures Trading Law
Thailand	Ministerial Order issued on September 16, 1992
Tunisia	Law No. 76–18 of 1976, as amended by Law No. 93–48 of 1993
Turkey	Banks Act
USA	International Banking Act
Venezuela	General Law on Banks and Other Financial Institutions

Note: WTO FSA country schedules.

Countries also listed their financial regulators in their multilateral liberalization schedules. Two-thirds (67%) of the signatories mentioned at least one specific financial regulator, and 37% mentioned two or more. The central bank and Ministry of Finance were the most common regulators listed. The next most common type of supervisor listed was in insurance, such as the Insurance Supervisory Authority, Bureau of Insurance, and Superintendent of Insurance. In securities, compared to banking and insurance, few separate regulators were included in the FSA schedules; many countries did not have separate securities regulators prior to the FSA negotiations (banking regulators often governed securities as well).[18] Some countries also listed nonfinancial regulators that affect financial services, such as the Ministry of Industry and Trade in Norway,[19] Lichtenstein's Parliament,[20] and the Minister of Health and Welfare in Japan,[21] who deals with financial licenses and employers' pension funds. Thus, through the FSA, entrants would now be able to easily find out host markets' existing and future regulatory developments. It would also help governments signal to foreign investors that they are committed to liberalization.[22]

[18] Some securities regulators listed in countries' FSA schedules were Securities Commission, Securities and Exchange Board, and Capital Market Board.
[19] "The Ministry of Industry and Trade may grant exemptions from these rules [on national treatment]" (Norway FSA schedule, GATS/SC/66/Suppl. 1/Rev. 1, p. 3).
[20] "License granted to banks and financial companies according to Lichtenstein Banking and Financial Companies Act has to be approved by the Lichtenstein parliament" (Lichtenstein GATS Schedule of Specific Commitments, GATS/SC/83-A, April 15, 1994).
[21] "With respect to the assets of Employees' Pension Funds qualified by the Minister of Health and Welfare to be managed by discretionary investment management service suppliers" (Japan's FSA schedule, GATS/SC/46/Suppl. 3, p. 7).
[22] Büthe and Milner 2008; Malesky and Milner 2021.

DE JURE LIBERALIZATION 97

Through these two mechanisms of creating a new international regime and a central depository of financial regulations, the FSA laid out specific norms of liberalization and independent regulation, and also reduced information asymmetry and transaction costs, which facilitated financial globalization.

5.2 Did Countries Change Their Financial Regulations?

This section examines the regional distribution of countries' adoption of the FSA norms of liberalization and independent regulation in their regulatory reforms. To determine how many countries have updated their regulations according to their FSA commitments, I created a database of domestic financial regulations on foreign entry and independent financial regulators in 148 countries from 1998 to 2007 (between the FSA negotiations and the global financial crisis).[23] I coded whether countries (1) lowered entry regulations and (2) created or strengthened independent regulators that reflect the FSA norms of liberalized foreign entry and independent regulation. I used a variety of resources to collect domestic regulatory changes around the world, including the WTO *Trade Policy Review*, laws and guidance of each signatory's finance ministry and central bank, and international law firms' reviews of global financial regulations. This database also expands existing databases of financial services trade restrictions, such as the Organisation for Economic Co-operation and Development's (OECD's) Services Trade Restrictiveness Index database, which covers 44 countries from 2014, and the World Bank's Deep Trade Agreements database, which focuses on preferential trade agreements, by including multilateral commitments and domestic reforms between 1998 and 2007 (before the global financial crisis) for 148 countries.[24]

Figure 5.1 displays the percentage of countries that liberalized their regulations on foreign entry (left) and strengthened independent regulation (right) in the banking industry within 10 years of joining the FSA. It shows that close to 120 countries, or over 80% of the signatories, have updated their regulations to match the promises made in the FSA to liberalize entry

---

[23] I narrowed the scope to 2007 to exclude crisis-induced regulatory changes after the 2007–2008 global financial crisis.
[24] Hofmann et al. 2017.

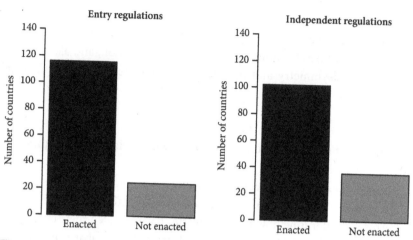

Figure 5.1 Liberalization of regulations on foreign entry and strengthened independent regulation in banking, 1997–2007.

barriers in banking, and over 100 countries have strengthened independent regulation in banking by either creating independent regulators or separating the regulatory function from the Ministry of Finance or central bank.

I next examine countries in Latin America and East Asia to determine whether (and how) the FSA led to substantial financial regulatory reforms in the key markets of interest to MFCs.

5.2.1 Latin America

Since colonial times, MFCs from the UK, US, Spain, and Portugal have entered Latin American countries, following their clients—traders and agricultural and manufacturing firms. MFCs stayed in the region even after independence, although countries in the region (such as Argentina, Brazil, Chile, and Mexico) oscillated between financial market liberalization and centralization as populist leaders came and went and financial crises peaked and subsided.[25] The high economic growth in the 1980s attracted more

---

[25] For example, Chile nationalized its private banks between 1970 and 1977 as part of the left-wing Allende administration's socialist program of *Unidad Popular* (Popular Unity). For Latin American countries' financial regulation history, see Inostroza 1979; McKinnon 1982; Velasco 1991; Lopez-de Silanes and Zamarripa 1995; Biglaiser and Brown 2005.

investment to the region. Petrodollars from the Middle East and US capital looking for high returns started to flow into Latin America, boosting investments in all economic sectors.[26] However, a series of inflation-adjusting measures in developed countries in the 1980s, such as the Volcker shock in the US, triggered a debt crisis in Latin America. The US government had to bail out American banks with overextended loans, and the International Monetary Fund (IMF) prescribed the Washington Consensus policies, which included trade and capital liberalizations, to Latin American countries during what became known as the "lost decade."[27]

A decade later, the FSA further opened up Latin American countries: 42 countries from the region had signed the agreement by 1997 and implemented substantial regulatory reforms in the financial industry after joining the FSA. Table 5.3 lists selected countries in Latin America that created or amended regulations on foreign entry that legalized the FSA norms of liberalization and nondiscrimination in banking, insurance, and securities within ten years of joining the FSA. It illustrates that all but one (Colombia) created or liberalized regulations on foreign entry in banking, and around 75% liberalized their markets in insurance and securities.

Table 5.3 Regulatory Changes Related to Foreign Entry and Liberalization in Latin America, 1997–2007

Reform	Banking	Insurance	Securities
Argentina	Y	Y	N
Bolivia	Y	Y	Y
Brazil	Y	Y	Y
Chile	Y	Y	Y
Colombia	N	N	N
Dominican Republic	Y	Y	Y
Ecuador	Y	Y	N
Guatemala	Y	N	Y
Honduras	Y	Y	Y
Mexico	Y	Y	Y
Nicaragua	Y	N	Y
Panama	Y	Y	Y

Sources: WTO *Trade Policy Review* and domestic financial regulations.

[26] Sims and Romero 2013.
[27] US treasury secretary Nicholas Brady proposed the Brady Plan in which the Department of the Treasury, IMF, and WTO helped reduce the debt burden of Latin American countries through debt reduction and rescheduling between 1989 and 1992.

100 MAKING FINANCIAL GLOBALIZATION

Some of the major economies in the region, such as Argentina and Brazil, legalized their FSA commitments. Argentina has traditionally had a large state presence in its financial industry[28] and a closed insurance market (it had previously suspended new entry in insurance in 1977).[29] However, after joining the FSA, it embraced multilateral financial services liberalization and created regulations that reflected its multilateral commitment to liberalization in the FSA. In 1994, in anticipation of its entry into the WTO the following year, Argentina removed the discriminatory treatment between foreign and domestic firms in its banking and insurance industries.[30] For example, it created new laws that "progressively eliminated" restrictions on foreign-owned banks (Decree 146/94 in 1994) and even allowed new enterprises to enter the previously closed insurance market (Resolution 25,804 in 1998).[31]

Argentina also started to privatize its pension and reinsurance business through Law No. 24,241 (Integrated Pension Fund System Law) in 1993, which attracted foreign insurers into the lucrative sector.[32] The US insurer MetLife entered Argentina in 1994 and attracted 300,000 customers within three years, generating an increase of $31.9 million in premiums and deposits.[33] However, Argentina still excluded state-owned enterprises from multilateral liberalization.[34]

Brazil, the region's largest economy, selectively opened its financial market through the FSA. The country has also long had a heavy state presence in the financial services industry: it has had a state monopoly in

---

[28] The largest bank in Argentina is the state-owned Banco de la Nación Argentina, followed by another state-owned bank, Banco Provincia de Buenos Aires, and foreign and domestic banks, namely Santander Rio, BBVA, Macro, and Galicia. See bnamericas, "At a Glance: Argentina's Top 10 Banks by Deposits," April 9, 2019, https://www.bnamericas.com/en/news/at_a_glance_argentinas_top_10_banks_by_deposits.

[29] "Authorization of the establishment of new entities is suspended" (Argentina's 1994 FSA Schedule, GATS/SC/4, pp. 14–15). Also see Clarke and Cull 2002.

[30] US Department of State, *1997 Country Reports on Economic Policy and Trade Practices: Argentina.* Submitted to the Senate Committees on Foreign Relations and Finance and the House Committees on Foreign Affairs and Ways and Means, January 1998, https://1997-2001.state.gov/issues/economic/trade_reports/latin_america97/argentina97.html.

[31] WTO *Trade Policy Review*, Argentina, Report by the Secretariat, October 2, 1998, WT/TPR/S/47/, p. 135.

[32] Borscheid and Haueter 2012.

[33] MetLife Form S-1, submitted to the SEC on November 23, 1999.

[34] "Financial operations by the Government and State-owned enterprises are excluded from the conditions specified in this schedule" (Argentina's FSA schedule, GATS/SC/4, p. 15). After Argentina restored the state pension plan in 2007, MetLife, which was the country's second-largest private pension insurer, sold its Argentine business to Grupo ST in 2021. In 2008, Argentina nationalized its private pension system through Law 26,425 during the global financial crisis. See A. Barrionuevo, "A. Argentina Nationalizes $30 Billion in Private Pensions," *New York Times*, October 21, 2008.

reinsurance since 1939. However, although it took nearly 20 years (it was one of the last original signatories to ratify the FSA in 2016), Brazil kept the regulatory promise it made in its FSA schedule to open its financial sector. Through the FSA, it allowed the entry of new financial firms, pending presidential approval.[35] Brazil committed to open its reinsurance markets to private enterprises 10 years after signing the FSA.[36] Indeed, in 2007, Brazil privatized reinsurance with Complementary Law 126 and started relaxing restrictions.[37] Brazil also submitted an updated liberalization schedule to the WTO in 2019 and engaged in meaningful liberalization efforts.[38] The Bolsonaro administration began to reduce state ownership in the financial sector in 2019 with the Law of Economic Freedom (Law 13,874), which reduced minimum capital requirements, among others, thus enhancing the business environment for domestic and foreign firms.[39]

Bolivia, Chile, the Dominican Republic, Mexico, and Panama, also created new regulations in banking, insurance, and securities. Mexico amended the Law on Credit Unions, General Law on Insurance, and Securities Market Law with regard to foreign entry in line with the FSA norms in 1999. Costa Rica and Nicaragua were fairly open to liberalization through the FSA; they listed a few restrictions on foreign entry and operation. Chile also removed discriminatory regulations in banking, insurance, and securities with the 1997 Banking Act, which equalizes regulations between foreign and domestic banks, and amended the Securities Market Act in 1999 and Law No. 20,190 (insurance) in 2007.

Other countries in the region were more restrictive in their multilateral financial liberalization schedules. El Salvador, Honduras, Peru, and Venezuela limited the share of foreign ownership to a minority stake at the time of the FSA signing. El Salvador limited foreign entry in the financial sector to a maximum of 25% ownership for non–Central American banks

---

[35] Brazil's FSA schedule, GATS/SC/13/Suppl. 3, p. 3.

[36] "Future regulations will permit supply by private institutions. Meanwhile, it is of the exclusive competence of the Brazil reinsurance institution" (Brazil's FSA schedule, GATS/SC/13/Suppl. 3, p. 3).

[37] Brazil's Insurance Supervisor, Superintendencia de Seguros Privados, "About Brazilian Insurance Market," http://www.susep.gov.br/menuingles/about_bim. Resolution 322 laid out a five-year plan to loosen the mandatory cession rule and intra-group prohibition. See Geoffrey Conlin, "Brazilian Regulatory Changes Good for International Reinsurers," Holman Fenwick Willan Law Firm Briefing, August 2015.

[38] UN Economic Development Division of the Economic Commission for Latin America and the Caribbean, *Economic Survey of Latin America and the Caribbean 2020* (ECLAC, 2021).

[39] "The New Brazilian Economic Freedom Act" (Hogan Lovells Publications, Brazil Law No. 13874 (Sept. 20, 2019).

102 MAKING FINANCIAL GLOBALIZATION

by requiring 75% ownership by Salvadorians or other Central American banks; Honduras limited foreign entry to 40% ownership; and Venezuela required a reciprocity of Venezuelan capital.[40] Peru went further, even prohibiting firms from using diplomatic channels.[41]

However, even countries that embedded restrictions in the FSA liberalized their financial market after the FSA. Peru liberalized its banking and insurance market and committed to the "prohibition of discriminatory processing" and the "non-participation of the state in the financial system" through the 1996 Law No. 26,702, the General Law of the Financial and Insurance Systems and Organic Law of the Superintendency of Banking and Insurance.[42] El Salvador, although it had limited foreign ownership in the financial sector, changed its domestic regulations (Law of Banks No. 697) in 1999 and subsequent years to allow 100% foreign ownership of foreign banks, which led to majority ownership by foreign banks, such as Citibank and HSBC, which became the second- and third-largest banks in the country.[43]

Many countries in Latin America have also made their financial regulators more independent. Bolivia, Colombia, the Dominican Republic, Mexico, and Nicaragua strengthened independent regulation in all financial subsectors—banking, insurance, and securities—within 10 years of joining the FSA (Table 5.4). Nicaragua enhanced its independent financial regulation through Law No. 316 (La Superintendencia de Bancos y de Otras Instituciones Financieras) in 1999. Colombia created the Colombian Superintendence of Finance through Law No. 964 in 2005.[44]

5.2.2 East Asia

The most sought-after markets and most contentious FSA negotiations involved East Asian countries. MFCs were attracted by the fast growth of Asian economies, especially China, Japan, Malaysia, and Thailand. However,

---

[40] El Salvador FSA schedule (GATS/SC/29/Suppl. 2); Honduras FSA schedule (GATS/SC/38/Suppl. 1); Venezuela FSA schedule (GATS/SC/92/Suppl. 3).

[41] "Foreign firms may not make claims through diplomatic channels, in respect of business or operations which they carry out in Peru, on the basis of rights derived from their nationality" (Peru's FSA schedule. GATS/SC/69/Suppl. 2, p. 2).

[42] Consolidated TPP Text – Annex III, Schedule of Peru, Section A.

[43] UNCTAD Investment Policy Review: El Salvador, 2010.

[44] IMF views this regulator as "operationally independent" (*Colombia Financial Sector Assessment Program*, IMF Country Report No. 22/135, 2022).

DE JURE LIBERALIZATION 103

Table 5.4 Regulatory Changes to Regulators' Independence in Latin America, 1997–2007

Regulator	Banking	Insurance	Securities
Argentina	N	N	Y
Bolivia	Y	Y	Y
Brazil	N	N	I
Chile	Y	N	N
Colombia	Y	Y	Y
Dominican Republic	Y	Y	Y
Ecuador	Y	Y	N
Guatemala	N	N	N
Honduras	Y	Y	Y
Mexico	Y	Y	Y
Nicaragua	Y	Y	Y
Panama	Y	N	Y

Sources: WTO *Trade Policy Review* and domestic financial regulations.

these countries had some of the highest levels of state control over the financial industry because they used financial repression to grow their economy by channeling domestic savings into industrial investment. Moreover, the Asian financial crisis made governments reluctant to fully liberalize at the WTO. After intense negotiations, governments in the region ultimately agreed to liberalize multilaterally through the FSA to bring back foreign investment for their domestic firms, but they did so selectively to control the pace of foreign entry.

Despite their fragmented liberalization through the FSA, however, East Asian governments did follow through with their domestic regulatory reforms after the FSA. In fact, they achieved some of the highest rates of domestic regulatory reforms of all FSA signatories. Table 5.5 illustrates that most countries in the region introduced new domestic financial legislation that reflected their FSA commitments.

Japan faced unending pressure to open up its financial market. At the time it was the second-largest economy in the world, and it had a surplus of savings and a closed insurance market, which attracted foreign insurers. In the insurance sector, the state-owned Japan Post Insurance had a strong grip over the profitable life insurance sector (the company sold insurance products through the national postal network). Foreign insurers, such as AIG, used multilateral and bilateral pressure to open up Japan's insurance market. Foreign pressure and the Japanese government's attempts to internationalize

104 MAKING FINANCIAL GLOBALIZATION

Table 5.5 Regulatory Changes to Foreign Entry and Liberalization in East Asia, 1997–2007

Reform	Banking	Insurance	Securities
China	Y	Y	Y
Hong Kong	Y	Y	N
India	N	Y	N
Indonesia	Y	Y	Y
Japan	Y	Y	Y
Korea	Y	Y	Y
Malaysia	Y	Y	Y
Philippines	Y	Y	Y
Singapore	Y	Y	Y
Thailand	Y	Y	Y
Vietnam	Y	Y	Y

Sources: WTO *Trade Policy Review* and domestic financial regulations.

its financial industry led to the financial system reform known as the "Japanese Big Bang." Under the three principles of "free, fair, and global," Japan enacted the Financial System Reform Law, which revised the Banking Law, the Securities and Exchange Law, and the Insurance Business Law, in 1998.[45] It also created a new independent financial regulator in banking, insurance, and securities—the Financial Supervisory Agency—in 2000.[46]

Korea was also going through a tumultuous time in its financial liberalization at the time of the FSA negotiations. Just a year prior, it had acceded to the OECD and committed to liberalize its financial market.[47] However, the following year, it faced the balance of payments crisis during the Asian financial crisis, and thus offered little liberalization through the FSA. Although the US held its IMF emergency funding hostage in return for financial liberalization, Korea committed less liberalization multilaterally than the prevailing domestic regulations at the time, citing its upcoming presidential election.[48] While Korea's final offer did remove the economic needs test (foreign entrants have to show how their entry satisfies the economic needs of host markets), it still fell short of foreign firms' demands, especially in insurance and securities.[49] However, just 15 days after the FSA passed, Korea

[45] Japan Financial Service Authority, "Japanese Big Bang," 2000.
[46] Japan's Financial Supervisory Agency and the Ministry of Finance's Financial System Planning Bureau merged in 2000 to form the current regulator, Financial Services Agency.
[47] WTO Committee on Trade in Financial Services, Report of the Meeting Held on 5 June 1997, June 20, 1997, S/FIN/M/14, p. 3.
[48] USITC 1998.   [49] USITC 1998.

established an independent financial regulator, the Financial Supervisory Services, through the 1998 Establishment of Financial Supervisory Act. It also liberalized its financial market by amending the Banking Act shortly after the FSA conclusion in January 1998 and the Insurance Business Act in 2003, and by passing the Financial Investment Services and Capital Markets Act in 2007.

Southeast Asian countries, such as Thailand, Malaysia, Indonesia, and the Philippines, were also of particular interest to MFCs because of the region's fast economic growth. However, these governments wanted to maintain local control over the financial industry while allowing foreign capital into their economies. After the currency crisis and capital flight that triggered the Asian financial crisis, governments were hesitant to liberalize further. They joined the FSA but with restrictive liberalization commitments.

Malaysia's FSA negotiation was the most contentious of all: its insurance schedule capped existing foreign ownership at 49%, which would force some foreign financial firms to divest, including AIG, which owned 100% of its subsidiary in the country, as discussed in Chapter 3. AIG did not give up and negotiated directly with Malaysia. Six months later, it cut a deal to invest $2.5 billion in the country and the Southeast Asian region; in return, Malaysia allowed AIG to grandfather its 100% ownership for another five years.[50] Malaysia did liberalize its insurance market five years later, when it increased its foreign ownership requirement from minority to majority share (51%) in 2006.[51]

The Philippines announced to the WTO GATS Interim Group on Financial Services meeting that it opened its market widely by passing the 1994 Banking Act, which "abolished a very restrictive regime that had been in place for nearly 50 years; access would now be allowed for foreign banks through the acquisition of 60% of the voting stock of existing domestic banks, through locally incorporated subsidiaries or via the establishment of a branch with full banking authority," and was opening its insurance market as well.[52] Indonesia liberalized close to what it specified in its FSA

---

[50] T. Fuller, "AIG Chief's Big Investment Pledge Delays a Sale of Local Unit: U.S. Insurer Cuts Deal in Malaysia, *International Herald Tribune*, May 5, 1998.

[51] "Branches of foreign insurance companies are required to be locally incorporated in accordance with the Insurance Act 1996 and foreign shareholding not exceeding 51 percent is permitted," Malaysia's Revised Offer, January 31, 2006, Council for Trade in Services Special Session, TN/S/O/MYS/Rev. 1, p. 36.

[52] GATS Interim Group on Financial Services – Note on the Meeting of 1 December 1994, S/IGFS/2, p. 2.

106 MAKING FINANCIAL GLOBALIZATION

schedule: it committed to eliminate its minority ownership restrictions in the nonbanking financial sector by 2020: "All Market Access and National Treatment limitations specified in the Non-Banking Financial Services Sub-sector will be eliminated by the year 2020 subject to similar commitment by other members."[53] Indeed, 20 years later, in 2018, Indonesia increased its foreign ownership to 80%, and in 2020 it allowed foreign enterprises that already had more than 80% ownership to maintain their existing ownership shares; however, it did not remove all ownership restrictions as promised through the FSA.[54]

Many East Asian countries updated their regulations to either create or strengthen independent regulators. Table 5.6 shows that the Philippines, Singapore, and Thailand all created or strengthened independent regulators in banking, insurance, and securities within 10 years of joining the FSA. Indonesia also made the Bank of Indonesia independent, "free from any interference of the Government and or other parties," and created an independent Financial Supervisory Authority.[55] However, India and Vietnam, which had large state-owned financial firms, did not liberalize immediately following the FSA: India increased the foreign investment limit to 26% in 2000, to 49% in 2016, and to 74% in 2021.[56]

Table 5.6 Regulatory Changes to Regulators' Independence in East Asia, 1997–2007

Regulator	Banking	Insurance	Securities
China	Y	Y	Y
Hong Kong	Y	Y	N
India	N	Y	N
Indonesia	N	Y	Y
Japan	Y	Y	Y
Korea	Y	Y	Y
Malaysia	N	N	Y
Philippines	Y	Y	Y
Singapore	Y	Y	Y
Thailand	Y	Y	Y
Vietnam	N	N	N

Sources: WTO *Trade Policy Review* and domestic financial regulations.

[53] Indonesia Schedule of Specific Commitments, 1998, GATS/SC/43/Suppl. 3, p. 2.
[54] Government Regulation No. 3 of 2020; Government Regulation No. 14 of 2018.
[55] Indonesia Report by the Secretariat, May 28, 2003, *WTO Trade Policy Review*, p. 89.
[56] D. Dayal and K. Chatrath, "Increase in FDI Limit: Allowing Foreign Ownership and Control in Indian Insurance Companies," *Lexology Website*, 2021.

The FSA led to domestic regulatory reforms on foreign entry and independent regulation in the MFCs' sought-after markets in Latin America and East Asia. Countries have implemented regulatory changes that embody the FSA commitments. For instance, they have lowered their entry regulations as specified in their multilateral liberalization schedule and created or strengthened independent regulation. The next section examines domestic financial regulatory changes in the US and China after the multilateral opening through the FSA.

5.3 Regulatory Developments in the US and China

In this section, I investigate how the multilateral liberalization agreement (FSA) lowered domestic regulatory barriers in the US and China. This case study traces the feedback loop between an international framework and domestic regulations: how the regulatory barriers led to the creation of an international agreement, which then influenced domestic regulatory reforms.[57] Empirically, the US and China were the most important markets in these negotiations. The US has been the largest financial market in the world for over a century, and China has been the most desired financial market for entry since the late 1990s.

The US and China represent opposing cases in two main explanatory variables examined in this book: financial linkage and state ownership. In the typology developed in Chapter 2 (Table 2.1), the US represents "open liberalization," while China represents "protectionism." On financial linkage, the US ranks high (above the median) while China ranks low (below the median),[58] which indicates that US industries utilize financial services more intensely in their production than Chinese industries.[59] The US also has a low level of state ownership of finance, while China has a high level. While the US financial industry is mostly composed of private banks,[60] at the time of the negotiations over 95% of China's financial market was owned

---

[57] Lake 2009; Oatley 2011.

[58] From the highest to lowest financial linkage, the US ranked 24th (2.07) and China ranked 44th (1.42) out of 62 countries, averaged between 1995 and 1997.

[59] For a discussion of financial linkage, see Chapter 3.

[60] The exception is the residential mortgage market: the US Treasury Department has owned a significant share of Fannie Mae and Freddie Mac since the global financial crisis. See Congressional Budget Office 2020.

by state-owned financial firms.[61] China's four largest state-owned banks—Industrial and Commercial Bank of China (ICBC), Construction Bank of China, Bank of China, and Agriculture Bank of China—alone accounted for over 70% of the country's total banking assets in 1998.[62]

This section describes how MFCs sought to use the FSA to reduce domestic regulations in the US and China. American financial firms used the specter of multilateral financial opening through the FSA to lower entry barriers not only abroad but also at home, such as the 1933 Banking Act (also known as the Glass-Steagall Act). MFCs also used the FSA to pry open their most desired market (China), even holding the country's WTO accession hostage on opening its financial market. Over the next 20 years, China gradually deregulated its financial market and created independent regulators, in line with its FSA commitments.

5.3.1 Changing Financial Regulations in the US

Although the US has had an open financial market and independent financial regulators since the early twentieth century, large financial firms have wanted to repeal the Great Depression era regulation that separated commercial and retail banking (the 1933 Banking Act) for more than a half-century.[63] Initially, a US bank was able to offer both commercial and retail banking services. However, during the "roaring" 1920s an economic boom and lax financial regulations created excess credit in the economy, and banks were using peoples' savings to make risky bets in the financial market. When the asset bubble grew too large, the stock market crashed and lost a quarter of its value within two days in 1929 (and remained 89% below its peak for the next four years). Banks lost large amounts of money, including many

---

[61] Berger et al. 2009.

[62] Cho 1999. By 2019, large state-owned banks accounted for around 40% of China's banking assets (Yeung 2021).

[63] In the banking sector, the Federal Reserve, an independent regulator, was created in 1934. It governs large banking institutions (about 68% of the financial sector's assets), while state banking regulators govern state-chartered banks (around 32% of banking assets); See Sykes 2018. In the securities industry, the US Securities and Exchange Commission, an independent regulator, regulates securities firms. The insurance industry does not have a federal regulator but has state insurance regulators that are members of the National Association of Insurance Commissioners (NAIC). The US government has to request cooperation from the NAIC, as seen in the FSA schedule Annex on Insurance Regulation.

people's life savings. This exacerbated the financial crisis and eventually led to the Great Depression.[64]

The public fury over banks' irresponsible behavior led Congress to pass the 1933 Banking Act, which separated commercial banking from investment banking and prohibited commercial banks that were primarily engaged in depository banking from selling or underwriting securities, and vice versa.[65] This led to the breakup of large banks, such as JPMorgan, into two banks—a commercial bank (JPMorgan) and an investment bank (Morgan Stanley).[66]

After World War II, European and Japanese economies grew as they recovered from the war, and their financial firms expanded abroad to serve their existing clients and look for new clients; they competed with US financial firms. Large banks such as Japan's Sumitomo and Mitsubishi banks and Germany's Deutsche Bank were among the largest financial institutions in the world by the 1980s, which caused US firms' global market share to drop.[67] By 1989, only one of the top 36 banks in the world was from the US (Citibank, ranked 12th).[68]

US financial firms blamed their falling market share on the restrictions imposed by the Glass-Steagall Act. They claimed to be at a disadvantage because Japanese and European financial firms were not forced to separate their commercial and retail banking, and could therefore offer a broader array of financial services to their clients. European financial firms had long followed the universal banking model, and Japan had deregulated with its Financial System Reform Act in 1992, which allowed financial holdings across multiple subsectors.[69] Thus, US financial firms lobbied Congress for years to repeal this regulation.[70]

---

[64] For more information on the stock market crash of 1929, see Gary Richardson, Alejandro Komai, Michael Gou, and Daniel Park, "Stock Market Crash of 1929," Federal Reserve History, 2013, https://www.federalreservehistory.org/essays/stock-market-crash-of-1929.

[65] The act also created the Federal Deposit Insurance Corporation, which guarantees individuals' deposits up to $250,000. For more information, see Julia Mauses, "Banking Act of 1933 (Glass Steagall)," Federal Reserve History, 2013, https://www.federalreservehistory.org/essays/glass-steagall-act.

[66] Morgan Stanley, "The Founding of Morgan Stanley," https://ourhistory.morganstanley.com/stories/a-bank-built-on-integrity/story-1935-founding.

[67] Goldberg and Hanweck 1991. Gale Group, 2011, p. 361.

[68] Goldberg and Hanweck 1991.

[69] D. Nanto, Japan's Landmark Financial Deregulation: What it Means for the United States, CRS Report for Congress, 1999.

[70] US financial firms were able to integrate, but they did so in piecemeal fashion and through side routes. Section 20 of the Glass-Steagall Act allowed banks to be part of a financial firm as long as its principal focus was not underwriting securities. Federal Reserve, "Financial Services Modernization

110 MAKING FINANCIAL GLOBALIZATION

The road to repealing the Glass-Steagall Act, however, had many obstacles, since interest groups, such as small banks and insurers, feared further concentration of power in the hands of a few large banks. The Independent Bankers Association and the American Council of Life Insurance gathered to oppose the act's repeal.[71] It was difficult to reach a consensus, as each large bank, small bank, insurer, and securities firm was "so interested in protecting its own business and hurting its competitors" that they changed their positions several times, depending on how the proposed bills affected their interests.[72] This domestic gridlock dragged on for three decades.

US financial firms also utilized the FSA negotiations to create international pressure on the US government to repeal the Glass-Steagall Act. They exhorted to Congress that once the FSA passed, their competitors in Europe and Japan would benefit from the global opening, while they would be held back.[73] Then-congressman John L. Mica (R-FL) recalled the financial firms' pitch to Congress: "The financial industry put a full-court press on and said, 'Oh, we can't compete in other financial markets and other countries are doing it and it's going to be the end of banking and finance as we know it.'"[74]

US financial firms also encouraged foreign financial firms to submit public comments to the US Congress about repealing the Glass-Steagall Act. At a WTO meeting in April 1997, the US representative to the FSA negotiations recounted that "the Treasury Department was moving ahead in terms of proposing the removal of the 1933 Glass Steagall Act...they were examining whether some reform of the segregation of the financial markets was long overdue."[75] The representative also stated that the US Congress "was beginning to have hearings on the proposal and the debate was opened to comments from foreign participants in the U.S. market."[76] The US representative said he "hoped progress would be made regarding

---

Act of 1999 (Gramm-Leach-Bliley)," Federal Reserve History, November 12, 1999, https://www.federalreservehistory.org/essays/gramm-leach-bliley-act.

[71] Hendrickson 2001.

[72] Leslie Wayne, "Shaping a Colossus: The Politics; Deal Jump-Starts a Stalled Banking Bill," New York Times, April 8, 1998.

[73] Wagner 1999; Hearing before the Subcommittee on Trade of the Committee on Ways and Means House of Representatives Hearing on Draft Final Text of the Results of the Uruguay Round of Multilateral Trade Negotiations (Serial 102–81). 102nd Congress Second Session, January 23, 1992.

[74] Ryan Grim, "Lawmakers Regret Deregulating," Politico, September 25, 2008.

[75] WTO Committee on Trade in Financial Services, Report of the Meeting Held on 10 April 1997, April 29, 1997, S/FIN/M/13, p. 2.

[76] WTO Committee on Trade in Financial Services, Report of the Meeting Held on 5 June 1997, June 20, 1997, S/FIN/M/14, p. 3.

the Glass-Steagall reform and said that any reform achieved would be immediately available to foreign participants in the U.S. market."[77]

MFCs used the FSA to highlight the urgency of global competition in order to break the decades-long domestic gridlock. Betting that the FSA's passage would precipitate domestic regulatory changes, Citi, one of the pioneers of the FSA negotiations, merged with an insurer, Travelers, in early 1998, which the Glass-Steagall Act prohibited.[78] The merger made Citi the largest financial firm in the world that encompassed banking, insurance, and securities. Congress ultimately passed the Financial Modernization Act, also known as the Gramm-Leach-Bliley Act, in November 1999, which repealed the Glass-Steagall Act and removed the barrier between investment banking and retail banking. This law allowed firms to form financial holding companies that could own subsidiaries engaged in different lines of business.

Using the specter of the global opening through the FSA, US financial firms finally succeeded in repealing the Great Depression era financial regulation at home while opening up the rest of the world. This led to a frenzy of consolidation in the financial services sector around the world as financial firms merged to expand their geographic and business reach. The consequences of the act's repeal were revealed 10 years later when financial firms became "too big to fail" during the 2008 financial crisis. At the time, President Barack Obama noted that "by the time the Glass-Steagall Act was repealed in 1999, the $300 million lobbying effort that drove deregulation was more about facilitating mergers than creating an efficient regulatory framework."[79] Firms pulled out all the stops, including a multilateral opening, to dismantle the obstacles to their business at home and abroad. The next section examines how MFCs used the FSA to pry open their most desired market of interest—China.

5.3.2 Opening the Chinese Financial Market

China's market has always been highly sought after. When the Opium War forced open China to international trade in the early nineteenth century,

---

[77] WTO Committee on Trade in Financial Services, Report of the Meeting Held on 5 June 1997, June 20, 1997, S/FIN/M/14, p. 3.

[78] Mitchell Martin, "Citicorp and Travelers Plan to Merge in Record $70 Billion Deal: A New No. 1: Financial Giants Unite," *New York Times*, April 7, 1998.

[79] Cyrus Sanati, "10 Years Later, Looking at Repeal of Glass-Steagall," *New York Times DealBook*, November 12, 2009.

112 MAKING FINANCIAL GLOBALIZATION

foreign armies brought traders to ship goods such as tea, spices, and silk out of China. Foreign insurers quickly followed to help traders insure their goods in transit and storage.[80] The British East India Company founded the first foreign insurer in China, the Canton Insurance Society, by merging two British trading companies to insure their ships and goods.[81] The American insurer AIG was originally founded in Shanghai, China, in 1919 under the name American Asiatic Underwriters by an American, Cornelius Vander Starr, before it moved its headquarters to New York in 1939 during World War II.[82]

When the Chinese Communist Party came to power in 1953, the government sought to end all private commerce in China and nationalized all insurers into a state-owned insurance company—the People's Insurance Company of China (PICC). China's private insurance business was essentially nonexistent by the time of the Cultural Revolution in the late 1960s (it resumed after Deng Xiaoping's 1979 economic reform, *Gaige kaifang*).[83] The private insurance firm Ping An was established in 1988 in Shenzhen to insure property and marine insurance of exports.[84] Similarly, the republic had only one bank—the People's Bank of China (PBOC)—which served as both the central bank and a commercial bank for three decades after the founding of the republic. After the 1979 reform, the government created four state-owned banks—Agricultural Bank of China, Bank of China, China Construction Bank, and Industrial and Commercial Bank of China—which it used to channel investment into state-owned enterprises (SOEs).

China gradually transitioned from a socialist economy to a market economy, or what Deng Xiaoping called "Socialism with Chinese Characteristics." However, the government still maintained a tight grip on its strategically important and lucrative financial industry. Unlike in a capitalist economy, where the market determines prices, the Chinese government set

---

[80] Swiss Re, "A History of Insurance in China," Swiss Re Corporate History, 2013/2017, https://www.swissre.com/dam/jcr:eb1aba5f-05ca-4bd4-bfe6-d42a6ed6b8c5/150Y_Markt_Broschuere_China_Inhalt.pdf.

[81] These companies only insured European businesses; they did not accept Chinese clients until the 1860s. Swiss Re, "A History of Insurance in China; Feng and Nyaw 2010.

[82] Greenberg and Cunningham 2013.

[83] Swiss Re, "A History of Insurance in China."

[84] Ping An, "China's First Joint-Stock Insurance Company," Ping An Transformation Story, Chapter 1, Ping An Website, May 18, 2021. https://group.pingan.com/media/perspectives/Chinas-First-Joint-Stock-Insurance-Company.html.

DE JURE LIBERALIZATION 113

prices, including in the financial industry, such as insurance premiums.[85] The Chinese government went to great lengths to protect its SOFIs, on the grounds that they "play an important role in serving the real economy."[86] As a result, by the time of the FSA negotiations in 1997, state-owned banks accounted for 95% of the Chinese banking system, while domestic private banks accounted for 4–5% and foreign banks only 0.01%.[87]

Chinese SOFIs, however, also had some serious shortcomings, such as a high debt burden and technological backwardness compared to private enterprises. For example, they faced huge debts due to their loans to SOEs: almost 80% of SOE debt in China was to its banking sector.[88] Moreover, due to the lack of competition, SOFIs' financial technology lagged behind that of foreign banks, which provided faster and global financial services around the world. This ballooning debt and technological backwardness made the Chinese government weigh the costs and benefits of foreign entry—between potentially losing its control over the financial market and attracting external capital and technology to the Chinese financial market.[89]

MFCs became more eager to enter the Chinese financial market because the growing economy presented immense business opportunities. The Chinese stock market had been underdeveloped and closed to foreigners for so long that few Chinese firms had used equity financing: the value of total traded shares (% of GDP) in China was only 1/3 of the US in 1997 (38% in China, compared to 108% in the US).[90] Moreover, according to the OECD Input Output Database, China's financial linkage was quite low at 1.42, compared to the US (2.07), UK (2.29), and Brazil (3.23), which indicated a huge growth potential for the Chinese economy and its businesses.[91]

---

[85] The Chinese government now specifies a *range* within which firms can set prices. The State Council and PBOC specify a narrow band of base rates within which banks can set their interest rates (Elliott and Yan 2013).

[86] Liu Xiao, "China Plans to Strengthen Control over State Financial Institutions," *Caixin Global*, July 10, 2018.

[87] Berger et al. 2009.   [88] Wei and Wang 1997; Lardy 1998; McNally 2002.

[89] The foreign investors included Goldman Sachs, American Express, Bank of America, Royal Bank of Scotland, Temasek, and UBS. See Elliott and Yan 2013, p. 17.

[90] Data from the World Bank's World Development Indicators database.

[91] The real estate sector had the highest level of financial linkage (1.21). The Chinese financial industry is closely linked to the real estate industry. As people's wealth increased with the growing economy, they invested in real estate. The other top sectors with levels of high financial linkage are financial intermediation (1.21); wholesale and retail trade (0.74); transport and storage (0.72); computer and related activities (0.59); electricity, gas, and water supply (0.56); research and development and other business activities (0.48); renting of machinery and equipment (0.45); and public administration, defense, and compulsory social security (0.44).

114 MAKING FINANCIAL GLOBALIZATION

As the Chinese economy grew, foreign securities firms saw merger and acquisition opportunities for foreign firms as well as initial public offerings of Chinese SOEs. Hank Paulson, then-CEO of Goldman Sachs in the 1990s (and later the US treasury secretary), invested in building personal networks with high-level government officials in China, such as President Jiang Zemin and Premier Zhu Rongji, to open China's financial market.[92] Goldman Sachs was allowed to open its first representative office in 1994 and was invited to coveted privatization deals by the Chinese government, such as China Telecom and Petro China. Morgan Stanley formed a joint venture with the China International Capital Corporation in 1995. Foreign insurers, such as AIG, were also keen to enter and expand business in China because of the country's high domestic savings rate and lack of a private pension system.[93] However, since these firms were only getting business in piecemeal fashion through their contacts, they sought a way to more reliably access business.

MFCs used China's WTO accession as an opportunity to force open its financial market. Norman Sorenson, a former executive at AIG, American Express, and Citigroup (all of which are FSA pioneers), testified at a House Committee on Banking and Financial Services hearing on implications of China's Permanent Normal Trading Relations for the financial industry that "opening the Chinese insurance market to American companies will lead to significant increases in insurance and pension premiums for U.S. providers, exceeding 300%. This development will surely benefit the U.S. trade balance," in order to pressure the US government into extracting concessions from China in the financial market opening.[94]

Near the end of China's 15-year bid to enter the WTO, its accession was held up over "market privileges for a single U.S. firm: New York-based insurance giant American International Group Inc."[95] AIG, a pioneer of the FSA negotiations, had a particularly dire problem in China. It had been allowed to enter the country in 1992 as the first foreign firm to own 100% of

---

[92] Paulson 2015.

[93] J. Cumbo et al., "China Pension Reforms Lure International Investors," *Financial Times*, April 28, 2022.

[94] "According to the American Council of Life Insurers, although China has one of the highest individual savings rates in Asia, its citizens spend less on insurance than citizens of any of 28 U.S. states... Financial Services companies—banks, insurers, asset managers, securities firms, and similar entities–are now protected against government actions which would prevent us from providing a broad range of financial products and services across national borders or which would discriminate against foreign owned financial services." Testimony of Norman Sorensen, president, Principal International, in front of the House Committee on Banking and Financial Services, May 11, 2000. Archives/Financial Services Committee/US House of Representatives; Archive Press Releases.

[95] C. Chandler, "AIG Dispute Keeps China Out of WTO," *Washington Post*, September 7, 2001.

its enterprise in China. However, through the FSA, China proposed capping foreign ownership in life insurance at 50%, which would have forced AIG to divest half of its business.[96] To prevent this from happening, AIG donated US$1.5 million to both Democrats and Republicans, with the key demand of opening China's financial market; the company even pressured politicians to block China's WTO accession until it further liberalized its insurance market.[97] Not wanting to be left behind, the EU also demanded that China allow wholly foreign ownership for European firms as well.

The negotiation over AIG ownership in China became so intense that Premier Zhu Rongji characterized AIG as "the only obstacle to China's WTO accession." He asserted that "if this obstacle is removed, I believe China will become a WTO member in November."[98] After intense negotiations, AIG president Maurice Greenberg and Premier Zhu Rongji cut a deal that allowed China to keep its 50% limit on the foreign equity share of life insurers but granted AIG an exception to grandfather its existing branches at 100% (it would have to find a 50–50 joint venture partner for future operations).[99] With that, China's WTO accession was cleared by the US; it joined in 2001.[100] AIG, as in the global FSA negotiations discussed in Chapter 3, had the last word over China's WTO accession.

5.3.2.1 Why (and How) China Opened Its Financial Market Multilaterally

China gradually opened its financial market despite the heavy international pressure for it to do so more rapidly. It modernized its financial industry and created independent regulators but still kept its control over the market. It opened just enough to help its exporters access global financial services and capital and upgrade its financial industry, but not enough for MFCs to establish a strong foothold in the country.

---

[96] K. Legget, "AIG Under Pressure to Sell Part of its China Operation," *Wall Street Journal*, September 5, 2001.

[97] G. Winestock, "AIG Is Key Issue Blocking China's Entry to the WTO," *Wall Street Journal*, July 19, 2001.

[98] C. Chandler, "AIG Dispute Keeps China Out of WTO," *Washington Post*, Sept. 7. China eventually allowed AIG's 100% ownership in life insurance while keeping the 50% limit on foreign ownership with the promise of future liberalization. See Geoff Winestock and Karby Leggett, "Negotiators Reach Accord on China's Entry to WTO," *Wall Street Journal*, September 17, 2001.

[99] CNN, "China in 'AIG Compromise,'" December 10, 2001.

[100] Winestock, "AIG Is Key Issue."

116 MAKING FINANCIAL GLOBALIZATION

China's multilateral financial services liberalization schedule illustrates its intention to open its financial market for its exporting firms while keeping the local financial market closed to foreign entry until its domestic financial firms were ready to compete. Figure 5.2 displays an excerpt of China's FSA schedule, which contains a section labeled "Clients," in which the government specified the types of clients foreign financial firms could serve in China.[101] The Chinese government allowed foreign insurers to serve only foreign enterprises in China for the first two years before allowing them to serve local clients.[102] It also limited foreign entry into the local currency market—a "market segment that foreign banks are most eager to pursue in China, particularly with regard to Chinese individuals."[103]

The Chinese government also phased in ownership and geographic restrictions to help domestic financial firms adjust to liberalization. It did not allow wholly owned securities firms to enter; only joint ventures with domestic firms were permitted, and foreign ownership was capped at 33%.[104] China took a gradual approach to geographic liberalization. It initially opened only four cities to foreign enterprises (Shanghai, Shenzhen, Tianjin, and Dalian), and then opened another five cities per year until it removed all restrictions within five years of accession.[105]

After joining the WTO, the Chinese government legalized its multilateral commitments in two steps through domestic regulatory reforms and independent regulation as written in its FSA liberalization schedule. First, the State Council, the country's highest decision-making body, created and revised financial regulations to institutionalize its multilateral liberalization commitments in banking, insurance, and securities through the FSA. In banking, it committed to allow foreign-funded banks to conduct business

---

[101] China's FSA schedule, GATS/SC/135, p. 34.

[102] Foreign financial institutions could only provide services to enterprises within two years after accession. Only after five years could they provide services to "all Chinese clients," including individuals. China does not have client restrictions for foreign currency business. "For local currency business, within two years after accession, foreign financial institutions will be permitted to provide services to Chinese enterprises" (China's FSA Schedule, GATS/SC/135, pp. 32–34).

[103] China allowed foreign entry into the local currency market five years after its WTO accession. See the WTO 2017 Report to Congress on China's WTO Compliance: Report of the United States Representative January 2018 at the WTO General Council (July 26–27, 2018, WT/GC/W/746, p. 23).

[104] "Within three years after accession, foreign securities institutions will be permitted to establish joint ventures, with foreign minority ownership not exceeding 1/3, to engage (without Chinese intermediary) in underwriting A shares" (China's 2002 GATS schedule, GATS/SC/135, p. 37).

[105] These five cities were Guangzhou, Zhuhai, Qingdao, Nanjing, and Wuhan. China then opened four more cities (Jinan, Fuzhou, Chengdu, and Chongqing) within two years, three more (Kunming, Beijing, and Xiamen) within three years, and another four (Shantou, Ningbo, Shenyang, and Xi'an) within four years before removing all geographic restrictions within five years of accession.

	Modes of supply: (1) Cross-border supply	(2) Consumption abroad	(3) Commercial presence	(4) Presence of natural persons
Sector or sub-sector	Limitations on market access	Limitation on national treatment	Additional commitments	
	B. Clients For foreign currency business, foreign financial institutions will be permitted to provide services in China without restriction as to clients upon accession. For local currency business, within two years after accession, foreign financial institutions will be permitted to provide services to Chinese enterprises. Within five years after accession, foreign financial institutions will be permitted to provide services to all Chinese clients. Foreign financial institutions licensed for local currency business in one region of China may service clients in any other region that has been opened for such business.			

Figure 5.2 Excerpt of China's FSA schedule. Shown is an explicit section on clients stipulating liberalization stages for MFCs serving their clients in China.

in domestic currencies five years after accession. Indeed, five years after its accession, China legalized this commitment by enacting the Regulations for the Administration of Foreign-Funded Banks in 2006.[106] China also kept its securities commitments in the FSA that allowed securities firms to establish joint ventures (up to 33%) three years after its accession through the FSA. Through the 2002 Establishment of Securities Companies with Foreign Equity Participation Rules, China legalized this commitment. This allowed Goldman Sachs to form a joint venture in 2004 (three years after China's WTO accession) with 33% ownership with China's Gao Hua Securities Company.

Similarly, in its insurance schedule in the FSA, China required foreign insurers to maintain a representative office in China for more than two years and to have total assets of at least $5 billion. China legalized this multilateral commitment through the 2001 Regulations on Administration of Foreign-funded Insurance Companies, which required foreign companies to have "no less than two years since the establishment of a first representative office in China; no less than US$5 billion in gross assets at the end of the year prior to application," among other requirements.[107] China also disbanded its "first and only" insurance company, the state-owned PICC, to "nurture more competition," and broke off life insurance to China Insurance, reinsurance to China Re, and property insurance to PICC Property Insurance company.[108] After China passed its first Insurance Law in 1995, more local Chinese insurance companies were established and foreign insurers entered as joint ventures, such as Chubb, Mitsui, Allianz, Aetna, and Prudential.[109] PICC separated its life insurance division in 1996, which became PICC (Life) and was later renamed China Life Insurance Company, which became the fifth largest insurance company in the world.[110]

---

[106] After incorporation, foreign-funded banks can offer domestic currency business only after demonstrating that they have had two consecutive years of profits in China (Regulations of the People's Republic of China on the Administration of Foreign-Funded Banks). The law allows foreign-funded bank branches to take deposits from (and make loans to) Chinese enterprises in domestic currency; branches can take deposits from (but *not* make domestic currency loans to) Chinese individuals (2017 Report to Congress on China's WTO Compliance. Report of the United States Representative January 2018, WTO General Council, July 26–27, 2018, WT/GC/W/746, p. 113).

[107] Trade Policy Review Report by the Secretariat: China, 2008, WT/TPR/S/199/Rev.1, p. 153.

[108] International Credit Insurance & Surety Association: PICC Property and Casualty Company Limited, https://icisa.org/member/picc-property-and-casualty-company-limited/.

[109] The Insurance Law was revised in 2002 after China's accession. Fang and Xu 2023.

[110] Fang and Xu 2023.

In a second step, the Chinese government legalized its multilateral commitment to establish independent regulators in banking, insurance, and securities. For decades, the central bank—PBOC—regulated all financial subsectors. However, soon after joining the FSA, the government created a banking regulator (China Banking Regulatory Commission, CBRC) through the 2003 Law of the People's Republic of China on Regulation of and Supervision over the Banking Industry; an insurance regulator (China Insurance Regulatory Commission, CIRC) through the 2002 Regulations of the People's Republic of China on Administration of Foreign-funded Insurance Companies; and a securities regulator (China Securities Regulatory Commission) through the 1998 Securities Law of the People's Republic of China.[111]

5.3.2.2 Post-FSA Financial Liberalization in China

As the Chinese economy grew, MFCs kept pushing China to open its financial market even further. One of the key restrictions in China's FSA schedule that MFCs wanted to abolish was the minority ownership requirement in insurance (50%) and securities (33%). The Chinese financial market, especially the lucrative insurance and securities business, was still relatively closed to foreign entry due to these restrictions. Thus, US financial firms continued to utilize multilateral and bilateral approaches to open China's financial market over the next two decades.

Bilaterally, MFCs utilized the biannual US-China Strategic and Economic Dialogue (S&ED), which was established as the Strategic Economic Dialogue in 2006 by US president George W. Bush (with the then-treasury secretary Hank Paulson) and Chinese president Hu Jintao and continued under US president Barack Obama and Chinese presidents Hu Jintao and Xi Jinping.[112] At these meetings, a contingent of Cabinet officials and business leaders traveled to each other's country to discuss long-term strategic and economic objectives. Financial business leaders lobbied intensively to raise the foreign ownership equity limits in China. After an S&ED meeting in

---

[111] CIRC was created in 1998 as a government division and became a ministry in 2002. The IMF calls CIRC "operationally independent," although it is subject to the direction of the State Council (IMF Financial Sector Assessment Program, Republic of China, December 2017, p. 16). In 2018, China further strengthened its financial supervision by merging CIRC and CBRC to create the China Banking and Insurance Regulatory Commission.

[112] CRS Report In Focus: "The U.S.–China Strategic and Economic Dialogue (S&ED): Economic Outcomes and Issues" (Congressional Research Service, July 14, 2015).

2012, China did raise its foreign ownership equity cap for securities firms from 33% to 49%.[113]

Although President Trump suspended these S&ED meetings, one of his first international acts within the first 100 days of taking office was signing a US-China economic agreement in which half of the provisions (5 of the 10) were related to opening the Chinese financial market for US financial firms, especially for Visa, Citi, and JPMorgan.[114] For example, the US asked China to allow "wholly U.S.-owned suppliers of electric payment services (EPS) to begin the licensing process," referring to the competition between China's Union Pay and US firms Visa and Mastercard.[115] Another provision asked China to "issue both bond underwriting and settlement licenses to two qualified U.S. financial institutions by July 16, 2017," which referred to JPMorgan and Citibank.[116]

A US industry coalition, the Coalition of Services Industries (CSI), kept pushing China to liberalize further and increase the foreign ownership limits for financial firms.[117] The CSI president testified in Congress that removing the equity cap in the insurance market had been "a top priority for the U.S. financial services industry for over a decade."[118] Finally, after more than 20 years, the Chinese government lowered restrictions in insurance and securities. It had kept its 50% ownership restriction in life insurance until 2020, when it increased its limit to 51% before abolishing it (thereby allowing wholly owned foreign enterprises). Germany's Allianz became the first foreign life insurer to own 100% of its Chinese business.[119] Similarly in securities, China increased its 20-year ownership restrictions from 33% to 51% before removing them completely.[120] Shortly after, foreign securities

[113] US Department of the Treasury, US Fact Sheet—"Economic Track of the Fourth Meeting of the US–China Strategic and Economic Dialogue (S&ED)," Press Release, May 4, 2012.

[114] US Department of Commerce, "Initial Actions of the US–China Economic Cooperation 100-Day Plan," May 10, 2017.

[115] US Department of Commerce, "Initial Actions."

[116] US Department of Commerce, "Initial Actions"; Sara Hsu, "Trump's Trade Deal 'Win' with China: Fake News?," *Forbes*, May 14, 2017.

[117] Reuters, "Foreign Insurers Gain in China Amid Scrutiny of Riskier Local Products," March 19, 2018. Only AIG had been granted 100% ownership. Geoff Winestock, "AIG is Key Issue Blocking China's Entry to the WTO," *Wall Street Journal*, July 19, 2001.

[118] Prepared Testimony of Christine Bliss, President, CSI, before the Senate Finance Subcommittee on International Trade, Customs, and Global Competitiveness, *Market Access Challenges in China*, April 11, 2018.

[119] C. Leng and B. Goh, "Allianz Becomes First Wholly Foreign-Owned Life Insurer in China," *Insurance Journal*, November 17, 2021.

[120] Xinhua, "China Lifts Foreign Ownership Limits on Securities, Fund Management Firms," April 1, 2020.

DE JURE LIBERALIZATION 121

vied to enter China to tap into its $44 trillion securities market.[121] JPMorgan became the first fully foreign owned brokerage, quickly followed by UBS, Nomura, and Goldman Sachs.[122]

Insurance also followed suit. The long-awaited opening of the private pension market finally occurred in 2022 when China created a private pension system (it initially only had a national social security system and corporate annuities).[123] This led multinational asset managers, such as Blackrock, Fidelity, and JPMorgan, to apply to offer individual retirement accounts to Chinese citizens, similar to the private individual retirement account system in the US. Given that China has an aging population, the market is expected to grow to $1.7 trillion.[124]

In addition to working through the US government, financial firms also utilized the WTO dispute settlement mechanism to open the Chinese financial market to foreign entry: 80% of the WTO disputes in trade in financial services (four out of five disputes) have involved China. The first three WTO disputes involved Xinhua, which is both a state-run news agency and the financial information regulator. It enjoyed a monopoly over the distribution of financial information in China; foreign financial news companies such as Reuters, Dow, and Bloomberg called this practice discriminatory, as they wanted to distribute information directly to local customers and not through Xinhua.[125] MFCs therefore pushed the US government to break Xinhua's monopoly over financial news distribution. When China did not change its practice, the US, EU, and Canada brought it to the WTO dispute settlement panel, where the parties reached a compromise: China agreed to create a new independent regulator of financial information, separate from Xinhua, and to allow the entry of foreign news service providers.[126] In 2009, China issued the "Provisions on Administration of Provision of Financial Information Services in China by Foreign Institutions," moved the approval authority

---

[121] BloombergNews, "China Will Scrap Securities Firm Ownership Limits by 2020, Li Says," July 1, 2019.

[122] Reuters, "JPMorgan Gets Beijing's Approval for First Fully Foreign-Owned Brokerage," April 6, 2021.

[123] Selena Li and Jason Xue, "JPMorgan, UBS and Others Vie for Bigger Share of China's Pension Market," Reuters, November 30, 2022.

[124] Reuters, "China Broadens Private Pension with New Participants, Products," November 18, 2022.

[125] Alan Wheatley, "Europe and U.S. Plan WTO Complaint against China on Financial News," *New York Times*, March 2, 2008.

[126] China—Measures Affecting Financial Information Services and Foreign Financial Information Suppliers (WT/DS373/4 S/L/320/Add.1, 9 December 2008); Reuters, "China Info Deal Creates Independent Regulator—EU," November 13, 2008.

122 MAKING FINANCIAL GLOBALIZATION

from Xinhua to the State Council Information Office, and allowed foreign companies to provide news directly.[127]

The fourth dispute in trade in financial services involving China was about the Chinese state-owned credit card company, Union Pay, which has been quickly growing as a competitor to US credit card companies such as Visa, Mastercard, and American Express. The US credit card companies have long tried to break into the Chinese market, which could potentially unlock opportunities for half a billion cards and trillions of transactions (and billions of dollars in associated fees).[128] However, the Chinese government has sought to protect Union Pay and kept foreign credit card companies out. As Union Pay increased its market share domestically as well as internationally, the US sued China at the WTO in 2010 on the grounds that China only allowed Union Pay to offer services in the local currency and limited foreign service providers to foreign currency business.[129] The panel found that China did keep Union Pay's monopoly over some (but not all) local currency denominated credit card transactions.[130] China promised to open its credit card company market to comply with the WTO ruling. However, it has been accused of obstructing the processing of entry applications for years. American Express was approved to offer its own cards in China only in 2020, and Mastercard's application was approved in November 2023. Union Pay has now overtaken Visa as the largest credit card company in the world, while US credit card companies have barely made a dent in the Chinese market.[131] China processes about $434 trillion in electronic transactions per year.[132] As Chinese financial firms have become the largest firms in the world, the US-China rivalry in financial services is expected to continue, bilaterally or multilaterally.

---

[127] Webster 2013.

[128] D. Palmer and F. Tang, "China Slow-walks Opening Country to U.S. Credit Card Companies," *Politico*, April 2, 2019.

[129] USTR. 2011. "China-Certain Measures Affecting Electronic Payment Services (DS413). First Written Submission of the United States of America." Sept. 13, 2023. https://tinyurl.com/mvyp34ms.

[130] World Trade Organization, *China: Certain Measures*.

[131] Statista, "Biggest Payment Card Brands—Visa, Mastercard, or In-market Local Card Schemes—in China from 2016 to 2020," March 2022.

[132] M. Toh, "Mastercard Will Soon Be Widely Accepted in China," CNN, November 21, 2023.

5.4 Conclusion

This study established that international agreements can be effective at changing states' behavior, such as altering domestic regulations in line with internationally agreed norms and principles. It showed that countries engaged in subsequent regulatory reforms to adopt the FSA norms of independent regulation, reducing state influence in the market, and lowering entry barriers. The agreement created an international depository of regulations and a new regime that established norms, principles, rules, and procedures in trade in financial services. These findings indicate that such agreements can lead to domestic regulatory changes.

It also examined how MFCs succeeded in lowering regulations in two major financial markets—the US and China. In the US, firms used the global financial opening created by the FSA to repeal the 1933 Banking Act (Glass-Steagall), which separated commercial banking from investment banking. This repeal led to mega-mergers and consolidations in the financial industry and allowed financial firms to cross over to many different financial businesses. By allowing banks to take excessive risks, it had more significant consequences for the global financial system a decade later during the 2007–2008 global financial crisis.[133]

The FSA also had far-reaching geopolitical consequences, including cracking open the long-closed and much-desired Chinese financial market. Because of the immense potential of China's banking, insurance, and securities businesses, foreign firms utilized every possible approach to open the country's market, even holding its WTO accession hostage.[134] China gradually opened its financial market to help its exporter business and created separate regulators in banking, insurance, and securities, in keeping with the FSA norms.

However, China maintained close control over its financial industry while liberalizing. It still "imposes substantial asset and capital requirements on foreign banks that it does not apply to domestic banks."[135] The six largest

---

[133] Ryan Grim, "Lawmakers Regret Deregulating," *Politico*, September 25, 2008.

[134] Elizabeth Olson and Joseph B. Treaster, "Insurance Seems the Hinge on China's W.T.O. Entry," *New York Times*, September 11, 2001.

[135] 2017 Report to Congress on China's WTO Compliance. Report of the United States Representative January 2018, WTO General Council, July 26–27, 2018. WT/GC/W/746, p. 23.

state-owned banks—Industrial and Commercial Bank of China, Agricultural Bank of China, Bank of China, China Construction Bank, Postal Savings Bank of China, and the Bank of Communications—still control around 47% of Chinese banking assets, and the foreign banking share is less than 2%.[136] Foreign insurance also only accounts for 2% of the market.[137] The top four global financial firms with the most banking assets in 2023 were all state-owned Chinese banks—ICBC, Agricultural Bank of China, China Construction Bank, and the Bank of China.[138] Moreover, not all signatories complied. For instance, Brazil's regulatory processes were stuck in limbo for almost 20 years until 2016. The governments of India and Vietnam did not liberalize foreign financial firms' entry into their markets.

Nevertheless, even a quarter-century later, the FSA and its forum, the WTO, have proven to be useful to financial regulators even after its adoption, and financial regulators continue to discuss domestic regulations at the WTO. To complement international financial institutions such as the IMF for capital account liberalization and the Bank for International Settlements for financial system stability, the WTO became an additional forum for international regulatory cooperation in financial services by creating a niche for regulation of trade in financial services and the current account liberalization in financial services. Financial regulators continue to exchange information about their regulatory experiences at the WTO Committee on Trade in Financial Services, and other international organizations, such as the Financial Stability Board and the International Association of Insurance Supervisors, also joined these meetings to discuss financial regulatory developments.[139]

---

[136] IMF Financial Sector Assessment Program, Republic of China, December 2017; V. Bisio, "China's Banking Sector Risks and Implications for the United States," US–China Economic and Security Review Commission. "China Banks Dashboard: December 2022—Foreign Banks in China," Fitch Ratings, December 12, 2022, https://www.fitchratings.com/research/banks/china-banks-dashboard-december-2022-foreign-banks-in-china-12-12-2022#:~:text=China%20Banks%20Dashboard%3A%20December%202022%20%2D%20Foreign%20Banks%20in%20China,-Mon%2012%20Dec&text=Near%2DTerm%20Challenges%20to%20Persist,China%20in%20the%20medium%20term.

[137] Fang and Xu 2023.

[138] S&P Global, "The World's 100 Largest Banks 2023."

[139] For example, Canada and Australia submitted documents on their experiences of financial sector reform. Report of the Committee on Trade in Financial Services to the Council for Trade in Services, December 4, 2002, S/FIN/8, p. 1; WTO Annual Report of the Committee on Trade in Financial Services to the Council for Trade in Services, November 16, 2017, S/FIN/32.

This chapter established how an international agreement has shaped de jure liberalization through domestic regulatory changes and paved the way for financial globalization. The next chapter examines de facto liberalization—whether the lowered entry barriers increased cross-border capital flows (MFCs' ultimate goal in advocating the FSA).

6

De Facto Liberalization

Cross-Border Financial Flows

In this chapter, I examine whether multilateral lobbying to create an international framework and lower the entry barriers for foreign financial firms led to an increase in cross-border capital flows around the world. Examining the effects of the international agreement on capital flows helps understand why multinational financial corporations (MFCs) spent time and resources to lobby for an international agreement. However, the literature is divided on the effects of international agreements on capital flows. Some studies argue that states can use international agreements to signal a credible commitment to investors[1] and transmit information, and thus increase capital flows.[2] Others maintain that such agreements are ineffective because of their institutional weaknesses, such as a lack of enforcement power and selection bias, and thereby do not affect capital flows.[3] For example, prior studies have found that international agreements, including the General Agreement on Tariffs and Trade (GATT) and the World Trade Organization (WTO), free trade agreements, bilateral investment treaties, and International Monetary Fund agreements, have had mixed effects on economic outcomes.[4]

This chapter tests this argument. I argue that the WTO Financial Services Agreement (FSA) would increase capital flows as it lowered entry barriers that blocked capital flows. In the following sections, I first examine whether the FSA led to the international expansion of MFCs through mergers and acquisitions (M&As), particularly in East Asia and Latin America. I then empirically test whether joining the FSA increased cross-border capital flows for signatories compared to before joining. Since the countries that joined the agreement may be fundamentally different from those that did not join,

---

[1] Ahlquist 2006; Goldstein et al. 2007; Tomz et al. 2007; Subramanian and Wei 2007; Baier and Bergstrand 2007; Büthe and Milner 2008.
[2] Keohane 1984; Kim 2021.
[3] Downs et al. 1996; Rose 2004; Jensen 2004; Von Stein 2005; Chaudoin et al. 2018.
[4] Rose 2004; Tomz et al. 2007; Baier and Bergstrand 2007; Büthe and Milner 2008.

Making Financial Globalization: How Firms Shape International Regulatory Cooperation. Clara Park,
Oxford University Press. © Oxford University Press 2025. DOI: 10.1093/oso/9780197761816.003.0006

I examine signatories' capital flows before and after the FSA. I examine three types of capital flows: trade in financial services, portfolio investment, and foreign direct investment (FDI).

6.1 Increase of Foreign Banks around the World

In this section, I examine whether international financial firms expanded into markets that they negotiated to open. We expect that as the FSA lowered entry barriers, firms could enter more markets through merging with or acquiring firms with experiences in the host market. Indeed, I find that after the FSA lowered entry barriers in the financial industry, MFCs accelerated their international expansion, especially into their key markets of interest: East Asia and Latin America. Foreign banks jumped at the opportunity and expanded quickly into the fast-growing countries in East Asia. Table 6.1 displays the increase in the operation of the most active foreign banks in 10 countries in Asia just before and after the FSA (between 1997 and 1999). Most countries in the region—Indonesia, Malaysia, Singapore, and Hong Kong—experienced an influx of foreign banks. The table also indicates that the low-income countries in the region experienced a faster increase of foreign banks than their high-income counterparts, possibly because the high-income countries already had a substantial number of foreign banks even before the FSA (while they also saw an increase after the FSA). For example, the number of foreign banks in Indonesia and the Philippines more than tripled after the FSA, while for high-income countries such as

Table 6.1 Asian Countries with the Most Foreign Banks

Country	1997	1999
Indonesia	8	25
Philippines	7	24
Korea	20	27
Vietnam	9	15
Malaysia	8	13
Japan	27	32
Singapore	27	31
Hong Kong	29	32
Thailand	15	10

Source: The Banker, May 1997, pp. 83–86; May 1999, pp. 62–65.

128   MAKING FINANCIAL GLOBALIZATION

Table 6.2 Foreign Banks with the Largest Presence in Asia

Country	Bank Name	1997	1999
Belgium	Generale Bank	1	6
Canada	Royal Bank of Canada	4	5
	Bank of Nova Scotia	6	7
France	Banque National de Paris	6	10
	Credit Commercial de France	2	6
	Credit Agricole Groupe	1	8
	Credit Lyonnais	6	9
	Paribas	4	7
	Societe Generale	3	8
Germany	Deutsche Bank	8	10
	Dresdner Bank	4	9
	Westdeutsche Landesbank	3	5
Italy	Banca Commerciale Italiana	3	6
	Banca Intesa	0	7
Netherlands	ABN AMRO	8	10
	ING Bank	7	7
Spain	Banco Santander	4	5
Switzerland	Credit Suisse	3	6
	UBS	3	6
UK	HSBC	9	9
	Standard Chartered Bank	9	10
USA	American Express Bank	6	8
	Bank of America	9	10
	Bank of New York	5	7
	Bank Boston	4	7
	Bankers Trust	5	8
	Chase Manhattan Bank	8	10
	Citibank	9	10
	CoreStates Bank	1	6
	J.P. Morgan	3	7
	Nations Bank	3	5
	Republic New York Corp	3	6

Selected foreign banks that operate in at least 5 of the 10 largest economies in the Asia-Pacific.
Source: The Banker, May 1997, pp. 83–86; May 1999, pp. 62–65.

Hong Kong, Japan, Singapore, and Korea the increase was gradual. Table 6.2 includes some of the most active foreign banks in the region, including the pioneers of the FSA negotiations—Citi and American Express (each with 8–10 banks)—along with J.P. Morgan, Credit Suisse, and UBS that have doubled their presence within two years before and after the FSA.

Latin America also experienced an expansion of foreign banking after the FSA. Table 6.3 illustrates the increase in the number of foreign banks in the major economies in the region. Argentina and Brazil were the most popular

Table 6.3 Latin American Countries with the Most Foreign Banks, 1998–1999

Country	1998	1999
Argentina	17	36
Chile	12	26
Peru	4	17
Venezuela	13	22
Brazil	30	37
Uruguay	15	20
Colombia	25	28

Source: The Banker, January 1998, pp. 67–68; January 1999, pp. 56–57.

destinations in 1998 and 1999 with over 36 foreign banks. Argentina, Chile, Peru, and Venezuela experienced an almost doubling of the number of foreign banks within a year after the FSA. Table 6.4 shows that the most active foreign banks in Latin America were US banks, such as Citi and J.P. Morgan; Spanish Banks, such as Santander and BBVA.

6.1.1 Mergers and Acquisitions

Furthermore, the FSA not only facilitated the international expansion of financial firms but also the consolidation in the financial industry. The global deregulatory movement encouraged financial firms to merge with each other and acquire other financial firms to gain a competitive edge. US financial firms in particular entered a frenzy of M&As in the financial industry. The pioneers of the FSA, such as Citi and AIG, grew even larger: Citi merged with the insurer Travelers Group to become the largest financial services firm in the world at the time; AIG purchased another insurer, American General Corp, in what constituted the "largest insurance deal in industry history to that time" in 2001.[5] The investment bank J.P. Morgan bought the commercial bank Chase Manhattan in 2001 to become J.P. Morgan Chase; Bank of America was created from the merger of BankAmerica in California and NationsBank in Charlotte, North Carolina. Table 6.5 lists the mega-mergers of MFCs, such as HSBC, Deutsche Bank,

[5] Tribune News Services. 'AIG to Acquire American General.' Chicago Tribune. May 12, 2001.

130 MAKING FINANCIAL GLOBALIZATION

Table 6.4 Foreign Banks with the Largest Presence in Latin America

Country	Bank	1998	1999
France	Banque National de Paris	5	6
	Credit Commercial de France	2	3
	Credit Lyonnais	4	7
	Societe Generale	3	4
Germany	Commerzbank	2	4
	Deutsche Bank	5	7
	Westdeutsche Landesbank	1	4
Italy	Banca Commerciale Italiana	0	7
Netherlands	ABN AMRO	5	6
	ING Bank	5	7
Spain	Banco Atlantico	2	4
	Banco Bilbao Vizcaya	5	7
	Banco Central Hispano Americano	2	5
	Banco Exterior de Espana	2	6
	Banco Santander	7	7
Switzerland	Credit Suisse	4	6
	Discount Bank & Trust Co	0	4
	UBS	2	7
UK	Barclays	3	4
	Lloyds	3	4
	Midland Bank	0	5
	Standard Chartered Bank	2	5
USA	American Express Bank	5	4
	Bank of America	5	5
	Bank of Boston	4	6
	Bankers Trust	3	6
	Chase Manhattan Bank	4	5
	Citibank	6	7
	J.P. Morgan	2	5
	Republic National Bank of NY	5	5

Selected foreign banks that operate in at least 4 of the 7 largest economies in Latin America.
Source: *The Banker*, January 1998, pp. 67–68; January 1999, pp. 56–57.

and Mitsui, in the financial industry between 1997 and 1999. The FSA and
the global financial opening led to fierce competition among financial firms
to grow larger and win more businesses.

6.2 Analysis of FSA Membership and Financial Flows

In this section, I examine whether joining the FSA increased signatories' cross-border capital flows. I argued in the previous chapters that
governments decided to join the international financial liberalization

Table 6.5 Major Mergers of Financial Firms

1996/97
Credit Agricole-Banque Indosuez
First Union-Signet
Wachovia-Central Fidelity
Bank Austria-Creditanstalt
US Bancorp-First Bank System
Swedbank-Foreningsbanken
GiroCredit-First Austrian

1997/98
Citicorp-Travelers
BankAmerica-Nations Bank-Barnett Banks
UBC-SBC
Banc One-First Chicago NBD
(First Union-Signet)-CoreStates
ING Bank-BBL
Wells Fargo-Norwest Corp
Bayerische Vereins-Bayerische Hypo
Generale Bank-ASLK CGER-Fortis Bank Nederland
Credito Italiano-Cariverona-Banca CRT-Cassamarca
Kredietbank-CERA
SunTrust Banks-Crestar
National City-First of America
Merita-Nordbanken
Cariplo-Ambrosiano Veneto-Cassa dei Parma e Piacenza
Den Danske Bank-Fokus Bank

1998/99
HSBC Holdings-Republic New York
Deutsche Bank-Bankers Trust
Bank Santander-Banco Central Hispano
Fleet Financial-BankBoston
Mitsui Trust-Chuo Trust
Firstar-Mercantile Bancorp
Den norske Bank-Postbanken
First American-AmSouth
First Security-Zions

Source: *The Banker*, July 1999, pp. 94–95.

agreement, even those without comparative advantages in financial services, despite the costs to their incumbent financial firms, in order to benefit from increased cross-border capital flows and an access to global financial services. Joining the FSA would signal to foreign investors that the country is open for business and will adhere to international economic laws. Furthermore, the lowered entry barriers (through domestic regulatory

132 MAKING FINANCIAL GLOBALIZATION

reforms) would ease cross-border capital flows. Therefore, I expect to find that FSA signatories received increased cross-border capital inflows.

6.2.1 Research Design and Data

The problem with studying the effects of an international agreement on economic outcomes is that countries that signed the FSA may differ from those that did not due to the selection effect. The counterfactual is that those that joined may have attracted capital even without the agreement; however, we do not observe this counterfactual in life. Furthermore, this agreement was not exogenous to countries' preferences, as governments and MFCs actively participated to create and shape the new international regime. Thus, I examine the within-country capital flow differences of the countries that joined the FSA, 10 years before and after the 1997 agreement (1987 to 2007) for up to 120 countries. This analysis is necessarily correlational and cannot establish a causal effect. I use two-way fixed effects analyses to control for constant unobserved country characteristics and common shocks over time. I estimate the following model:

$$Y_{it} = \alpha + \beta_1 FSA_{it} + \beta_2 X_{it} + v_t + \gamma_i + \epsilon_{it} \tag{6.1}$$

where Y_{it} is a set of cross-border capital flows—trade in financial services, portfolio investment, and FDI—for country i, at time t. FSA_{it} denotes country i's FSA membership at time t, X_{it} is a vector of country-level controls at time t, γ_i are country fixed effects, v_t are time (year) fixed effects, and ϵ is a white noise error term. All standard errors are adjusted to account for non-constant variances and within-country correlation of residuals.

FSA Membership. The main variable of interest is a country's FSA membership status each year. I create an indicator variable that equals 1 for years after a country joined the FSA, and 0 before.

Dependent Variables. I examine three types of cross-border capital flows: trade in financial services, FDI inflows, and portfolio investment. The first outcome variable is *trade in financial services*, which refers to the cross-border services provided by financial service providers, such as cross-border loan services, insurance brokerage services, or M&A services. Imports and exports of trade in financial services enter into the country's current account, which comprises trade in goods and services. Since the FSA lowered trade barriers, joining the agreement is expected to increase imports of trade in financial and insurance services.[6]

The second outcome variable is *FDI flows*, which the World Bank defines as "net flows of investment to acquire a lasting management interest (10 percent or more of voting stock) in an enterprise operating in an economy other than that of the investor."[7] The FSA lowers entry barriers and facilitate the entry of MFCs that follow their corporate clients into host markets, thus joining the FSA is expected to increase FDI. I examine both FDI inflows and outflows. Since countries liberalized their financial industry to attract foreign investment to their domestic enterprises, I examine whether FDI inflows did in fact increase. I also examine FDI outflows to determine if FSA signatories increased their foreign investments.

The third outcome variable is *portfolio equity inflows*, which includes "direct purchases of shares in local stock markets by foreign investors such as buying stocks in foreign companies."[8] MFCs' ultimate goal in seeking to establish a commercial presence in other countries was to facilitate cross-border portfolio equity investments. Therefore, I expect to observe an increase in portfolio equity inflows for countries that signed the FSA.

Control Variables. I also include a set of other time-varying explanatory variables that could affect both the likelihood of membership and cross-border capital inflows, such as the level of financial sector development, size of the economy, regime type, and share of exports. All control variables are standardized to have a mean of 0 and a variance of 1.

Financial sector development. A country with a developed financial sector is likely to sign the FSA and to receive more foreign capital. I use the standard variable employed in the international finance literature to measure financial sector development—domestic credit provided by the financial sector as a share of GDP (from the World Development Indicators).

Economy size. The size of a country's economy can affect its decision about whether to sign the international liberalization agreement: a rich country may be more likely to join because it is more likely to gain from liberalization. A poor country may either join the agreement to attract foreign capital or

---

[6] Data is from UNCTAD Data Center (BPM6: Exports and Imports by service category and trade partner, annual).

[7] World Bank, "Foreign Direct Investment, Net Inflows (% of GDP)," World Development Indicator.

[8] Portfolio equity inflows include "net inflows from equity securities other than those recorded as direct investment and including shares, stocks, depository receipts, and direct purchases of shares in local stock markets by foreign investors" (World Bank), World Development Indicator.

134 MAKING FINANCIAL GLOBALIZATION

not join it due to fears of losing control over its financial sector to foreigners. I measure the size of a country's economy as GDP per capita using World Development Indicators data.

Democracy. Several studies maintain that democracies are more likely to sign an international agreement and to attract capital flows due to their rule of law and property rights protection.[9] I therefore account for regime type by including Polity scores, which range from −10 (most autocratic) to +10 (most democratic).[10]

Exports. A country with a large export profile may be more likely to sign the FSA to facilitate its export businesses and attract more foreign capital. For the export measure, I use the share of exports of goods and services (% of GDP from the World Bank's World Development Indicators data).

6.3 Results

6.3.1 Trade in Financial Services

First, I analyze how the FSA has shaped trade in financial services. Table 6.6 reports the estimated effects of joining the FSA on imports of financial and insurance services trade (measured in million USD, logged) with country and year fixed effects. It establishes that joining the FSA increases trade in financial and insurance services imports by $220–620 million (0.441 to 0.665

Table 6.6 Effect of Joining the FSA on the Level of Import of Trade in Financial and Insurance Services: Two-Way Fixed Effects Estimates.

	Model 1	Model 2	Model 3
FSA	0.441*	0.665*	0.550*
	(0.116)	(0.278)	(0.247)
N	697	471	463
Extended Controls	no	yes	yes
Country FE	yes	yes	yes
Year FE	yes	yes	yes

Robust Standard Errors in parentheses.

* $p < 0.05$

[9] Li and Resnick 2003; N. M. Jensen 2008; Büthe and Milner 2008; Pepinsky 2013; Pond 2018.
[10] Data comes from the Polity IV database.

log points), after joining the FSA; these results are positive and robust across all three specifications at the 95% level of significance.

Model 1 controls for the size of the economy and regime type using GDP per capita and Polity scores. I control for a country's regime type (using Polity scores) because a democracy is more likely to sign an international liberalization agreement and attract foreign capital than an autocracy, since it is apt to have a rule of law that protects foreign investment. Similarly, a rich country is likely to sign an international liberalization agreement and attract capital. In Model 2, in addition to GDP per capita and the level of democracy, I also add specific variables for financial services, the country's level of financial development, and share of foreign banks already in the country; the latter could affect financial trade flows because the more developed a country's financial sector is, the more likely it is to actively participate in the financial market.[11] When foreign bank share, the level of financial development, and the level of exports are added, trade in financial services increases around $624 million (0.665 log points).

Model 3 employs a different dependent variable, the share of insurance and financial services in total imports, which indicates the importance of the financial sector as a share of total imports. In this specification, joining the FSA generates a 55-percentage-point increase in insurance and financial services as a share of the country's total imports. Countries that joined the FSA experienced a significant increase in trade in financial services in both absolute and relative terms compared to before joining.

6.3.2 FDI

Financial firms follow their corporate clients (for example, in the agriculture, mining, and manufacturing industries) that go to foreign markets for new factories and markets. Thus, the lowered entry barriers for MFCs through the FSA are expected to increase FDI flows of countries that joined the FSA from increases in internatioanl trade and global value chain integration. Table 6.7 reports the results of the within-country analysis of FSA membership on subsequent FDI inflows (Models 1–2) and outflows

---

[11] I control for the standard variable used in the international finance literature to measure the size of the financial sector—domestic credit to the private sector as a share of GDP. Data for these economic variables (GDP per capita, share of foreign banks, and the size of the financial sector) comes from the World Bank World Development Indicator database.

136 MAKING FINANCIAL GLOBALIZATION

Table 6.7 Effect of Joining the FSA on Changes in Total FDI (Inflows and Outflows): Two-Way Fixed Effects Estimates

	FDI Inflows	FDI Inflows	FDI Outflows	FDI Outflows
FSA	0.219*	0.233*	0.288*	0.324*
	(0.111)	(0.110)	(0.128)	(0.127)
N	1302	1274	1069	1041
adj. R^2	0.586	0.587	0.594	0.597
Extended Controls	no	yes	no	yes
Country FE	yes	yes	yes	yes
Year FE	yes	yes	yes	yes

Robust Standard Errors in parentheses.

* $p < 0.05$

(Models 3–4) with country and year fixed effects. Countries with any missing data are dropped, which produces a sample of 71 countries.

I find that joining the FSA leads to a \$2–3 billion increase in FDI inflows and outflows; these results are statistically significant across specifications at the 95% level. The first column presents the basic analysis of membership on FDI inflows, including basic controls for economy size (GDP per capita) and regime type (Polity score). It illustrates that joining the FSA leads to an increase of 0.219, or \$2.19 billion, in FDI inflows (values in million USD are divided by 10,000 for scale). The second column includes political, economic, and financial variables, as in the earlier analysis, and shows that signatories' FDI inflows increased by \$2.33 billion after joining.

The next two analyses demonstrate that countries also send out more FDI after joining the FSA. Signing the agreement leads to an increase of 0.288 (\$2.88 billion in FDI outflows) in Model 3 and a 0.324 increase (\$3.24 billion in outflows) after adding all control variables in Model 4. These analyses establish that the FSA signatories become more active in international investment, increasing FDI flows by \$2–3 billion compared to before joining. All results are statistically significant at the 95% level, and are comparable across inflows and outflows.

6.3.3 Portfolio Investment

Since the FSA facilitates the entry of foreign financial firms, countries that signed the agreement are more likely to receive portfolio equity inflows

Table 6.8 Effect of Joining the FSA on the Incidence of Positive Portfolio Equity Inflows: Linear Probability Two-Way Fixed Effects Estimates

	Model 1	Model 2	Model 3
FSA	0.168*	0.221*	0.221*
	(0.065)	(0.093)	(0.093)
N	1427	931	902
adj. R^2	0.234	0.134	0.139
Extended Controls	no	yes	yes
Country FE	yes	yes	yes
Year FE	yes	yes	yes

Standard errors in parentheses.

* $p < 0.05$

following the expansion of MFCs into their markets. Since portfolio equity flows are measured as net inflows, roughly half of the sample had either negative inflows (more outflows than inflows) or net zero inflows; the other half had positive net inflows. Thus, I model whether countries had positive inflows after joining the FSA (using an indicator that equals 1 if countries had positive inflows and 0 for non-positive flows).

Table 6.8 reports the coefficients of a linear probability model of the impact of joining the FSA on positive portfolio equity inflows with country and year fixed effects. In Model 1, joining the FSA leads to a 17-percentage-point increase in the probability of observing positive portfolio equity inflows when using standard control variables (GDP per capita, level of exports, and level of financial development). These results are statistically significant and substantially relevant. When adding more controls, such as FDI inflows per GDP, stocks traded per GDP, and regime type, the probability of observing positive portfolio equity inflows increases by 22 percentage points. Countries thus receive more portfolio equity inflows after joining the FSA.

Figure 6.1 summarizes the changes in all three types of capital flows before and after joining the FSA and the expected values calculated from the model. All other controls are held at their observed values. It shows that countries that joined the FSA experienced increases in capital flows, including FDI inflows, trade in financial services imports, and positive portfolio equity inflows, and the difference is statistically significant. FDI inflows doubled from about $2 billion to $4 billion; trade in financial services imports also

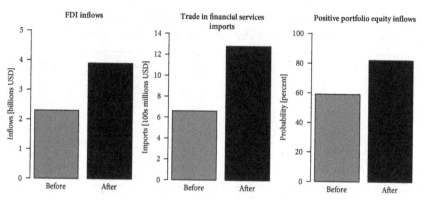

Figure 6.1 Changes in capital flows before and after joining the FSA. Expected values of FDI inflows, trade in financial services imports, and positive portfolio equity inflows, including all controls. Calculated from two-way fixed effects models shown in Tables 6.8.

doubled from around $610 million before signing the FSA to $1.3 billion afterwards (around a $620 million increase). The likelihood of receiving net positive portfolio equity inflows also increased from 60% to over 80%. MFCs worked hard to open the world market and succeeded in their goal of increasing capital market transactions.

6.4 Discussion

This chapter examines whether the international agreement in financial services increased financial firms' international expansion, M&As, and countries' financial flows. I find that MFCs increased their international footprints, including their commercial presence, especially in key markets of interest in East Asia and Latin America. They also enlarged through M&As to more effectively compete against each other in the global financial market. My within-country analysis reveals that joining the FSA increased cross-border capital flows—financial services imports, portfolio investments, and total FDI inflows—into signatory countries. Joining the FSA almost doubled trade in financial services imports by $220–624 million; membership increased FDI inflows and outflows by $2–3 billion and positive portfolio equity inflow by 22 percentage points.

These analyses demonstrate that the international agreement affected real-world economic changes. While it is difficult to establish the causal effect of the FSA on capital flows, since countries and MFCs actively participated in the negotiations and those that joined may be different from those that did not join in unobserved ways, we can examine the correlation of joining the FSA and changes in cross-border capital flows for the countries that joined over time. The analyses showed that countries that joined the agreement saw an increase in cross-border capital flows; joining the FSA signaled countries' commitment to liberalization, legalized their multilateral liberalization commitments with a dispute settlement mechanism, and provided information on their present and future regulatory reforms, as discussed in the previous chapters.

The FSA opened the global financial market, which allowed international investors to enter foreign markets and facilitate cross-border capital flows, short-term portfolio equity investment, and trade in financial services imports as well as long-term FDI. Countries that joined the FSA received an inflow of much-needed external capital into their markets. This analysis shows that MFCs' multilateral lobbying led to their desired outcome of facilitating foreign entry and increasing cross-border capital flows around the world.

7

Conclusion

We now take it for granted that we can use our credit cards in hotels and restaurants around the world and walk into a bank abroad to withdraw cash, but it has not always been this way. Many governments used to control financial markets and prevent foreign financial firms from accessing the country. Given the strategic and economic importance of the financial industry, many countries (including some developed countries) have had state-owned financial institutions (SOFIs) and entry barriers against multinational financial corporations (MFCs).[1] These entry barriers included which types of businesses were allowed (branches, subsidiary, or representative office) or how much ownership share was allowed (minority, joint venture, majority, or whole enterprise). Moreover, many countries did not have indepedent regulators in finance, but instead had a ministry of finance, which operated SOFIs, to regulate the entry and operation of MFCs. Thus, for decades, MFCs had to negotiate entry bilaterally and deal with discriminatory regulations in host markets.

In 1997, 102 countries signed the Financial Services Agreement (FSA) to liberalize their financial services trade, which is at the intersection of international trade liberalization and international financial liberalization. The FSA lowered the behind-the-border regulatory barriers in the financial industry and called for independent financial regulators. MFCs could now enter previously closed markets or expand their business beyond basic services, and cross-border capital flows increased around the world.

To explain the creation of this international framework and the resulting domestic regulatory changes, I have argued in this book that compared to the conventional wisdom of state-driven regime creation, it was the firms that pushed for—and shaped—the creation of an international financial services agreement (the FSA). The book presents the theory of financial

---

[1] France, Germany, and Japan have a historically large state presence in the financial sector. The US and UK have mostly private firms in the financial industry, although the US does have government-sponsored enterprises such as Fannie Mae and Freddie Mac.

Making Financial Globalization: How Firms Shape International Regulatory Cooperation. Clara Park,
Oxford University Press. © Oxford University Press 2025. DOI: 10.1093/oso/9780197761816.003.0007

globalization, which provides a framework with which to analyze firms' strategies in international negotiations on trade in financial services liberalization. As multinational corporations (MNCs) expanded abroad in search of cheaper inputs and new markets, multinational financial corporations (banks, insurers, and securities firms) sought to follow their MNC clients abroad and provide cross-border financial services, such as trade financing and marine and fire insurance. However, as they faced idiosyncratic entry barriers in foreign countries, financial firms engaged in multilateral lobbying to open up the global financial market. They sought to reduce information asymmetries and the transaction costs associated with bilateral bargaining processes through a multilateral agreement. To break down entry barriers around the world, firms formed coalitions across industries and countries to build an industry consensus to create an international liberalization framework and influence both home and host governments as well as international organizations.

This theory breaks down the preferences of major actors in international financial services negotiations: firms and governments. To explain firms' preferences in financial globalization, I introduced a new measure of financial linkage—the extent to which financial services are used as inputs in other industries and the economy's dependence on financial services—for firms that use financial services as inputs in producing their outputs in the agriculture, mining, and manufacturing industries (loans for machines, insurance for goods in transit, and equity stocks). I showed how such financial linkage pushed firms to expand abroad and governments to open their previously closed markets.

This theory also derived governments' preferences in financial services liberalization from its dual objectives: economic growth and market control. Governments face a dilemma in financial services liberalization. On the one hand, financial services liberalization will bring in external capital and technology needed for economic growth. However, it would also bring in powerful MFCs into their markets, and governments may lose control in the financial market to foreign firms. Thus, governments, motivated to attract foreign capital and global financial services that would help domestic businesses, signed the multilateral financial services liberalization agreement and gradually opened their markets to MFCs. However, at the same time, governments embedded various restrictions during liberalization to maintain as much control as possible over the pace of foreign entry into their financial markets.

142 MAKING FINANCIAL GLOBALIZATION

In Chapter 3, I tested the first step of my argument—whether countries with higher levels of financial linkage were more likely to join the international liberalization agreement on trade in financial services. I found that they were indeed more likely to sign the FSA, because such countries have more industries and firms that depend on financial services for their inputs, and liberalization would benefit their domestic champions. I also examined MFCs' international expansion strategies and industry coalition formation across countries and industries.

In Chapter 4 I investigated the second part of my argument—why countries joined the FSA but included restrictions. I hypothesized that countries with a high level of state control in the financial market were more likely to include restrictions to maintain as much control over the market as possible during liberalization. I found that these countries were more likely to include more (and more severe) restrictions, such as limiting foreign ownership to a minority stake and imposing higher capital requirements on foreign firms than domestic companies. These moves were designed to limit the reach of (often more efficient) MFCs that would threaten to erode the state's control over the financial market. Thus, governments included restrictions while liberalizing to control the speed and extent of foreign entry.

In Chapter 5 I analyzed whether the international agreement led to *de jure* changes in domestic financial regulations around the world. The FSA required countries to submit their plans to reduce domestic regulatory entry barriers. I used this information to create a new database on financial entry regulations in 148 countries, and coded whether countries changed their domestic regulations in line with their multilateral liberalization commitments. I compared their FSA schedules and domestic regulatory reforms to ensure they reflected countries' spescific FSA commitments. I found that the FSA did trigger domestic regulatory reforms: 92 countries changed their domestic regulations to adhere to their multilateral liberalization commitments.

I also evaluated the cases of the two most sought-after financial markets— the US and China—to trace the mechanism through which firms used the FSA to lower financial restrictions in both countries. In the US, financial firms used the specter of multilateral opening through the FSA to finally persuade Congress to repeal the 1933 Banking Act (Glass-Steagall Act), which had separated commercial banking from retail banking since the Great Depression. As European and Japanese financial firms began to rise in global market power, US firms viewed this regulation as inhibiting their international competition. They engaged in a decades-long legislative battle to repeal it but faced domestic roadblocks. The global opening through the FSA increased the urgency of the repeal, and firms' international and domestic efforts helped convince legislators this was necessary.

Firms also used the FSA to open up the heavily sought-after Chinese financial market. Beijing had long been hesitant to open its financial market, despite huge international pressure. Western financial firms even lobbied their governments to make China's WTO accession conditional on its financial services liberalization. China finally opened its financial market, albeit gradually, and created new financial regulators. While Beijing maintained close control over its market, it liberalized its financial market in accordance with its multilateral FSA commitments over the next 20 years.

Finally, Chapter 6 examined whether the FSA was effective—i.e., whether it changed actors' behaviors and economic outcomes. My analyses demonstrated that the international agreement significantly increased signatories' capital flows—trade in financial services, portfolio investment, and foreign direct investment.

This framework of multilateral lobbying and inter-industry linkages helps identify the major stakeholders and their preferences in international negotiations, as well as how they designed the scope, depth, and membership of agreements. Firms achieved their goal of expanding their business globally through the new international regime, which led to domestic regulatory reform and increased cross-border capital flows. Unpacking these layers of interests illustrates how firms created cross-industry and cross-country coalitions and interacted with their home governments, host governments, and international organizations.

The theory presents an analytical framework with which to trace the preferences of governments and firms as well as the role of industry coalitions in international policymaking. It complements three main explanations of international economic negotiations in international political economy: domestic politics, institution-based, and power-based explanations.

First, the theory unpacks the black box of behind-the-door international negotiations by tracing the sources of domestic interest groups' preferences, as in open economy politics. However, it goes further by showing how these micro-foundations shape the international political actions of firms and governments as well as macroeconomic outcomes. For example, I traced financial firms' interests back to their institutional clients, including firms in the mining, manufacturing, and telecommunications services industries, and

144 MAKING FINANCIAL GLOBALIZATION

demonstrated how firms formed coalitions across industries and countries, such as the Global Services Coalition. This framework builds on Putnam's two-level game (1988), in which he called on future researchers to explore "the strategic implications of direct communication between Level II players."[2] Indeed, by broadening the coalition of interested industries, I showed that even sectoral negotiations can gain support from other sectors in their global value chains that would directly and indirectly benefit from liberalizing industries.

Second, my theory rejects the conventional narrative of state-led regime creation and provides insights into firms' role in international policymaking. Since firms are at the forefront of commercial expansion, they experienced behind-the-border barriers. They chose the World Trade Organization (WTO) as the home for an international agreement to lower these barriers. Furthermore, firms supplied the language of the new regime, such as norms, principles, rules, and procedures, based on their experiences and desired outcomes. They exercised such a large influence over the agreement from its inception to conclusion because they operated in the realm of "quiet politics" (Culpepper 2010): the public was mostly unaware of the negotiations due to the low political salience of trade in services negotiations.

Third, this theory complements the power asymmetry argument by helping to explain how the US developed its preferences in international economic explanations, such as why the US was interested in opening up small financial markets with little business potential and why it was not able to get all of its demands in global financial services liberalization. In this study I explore the origins of US financial firms' preferences that shaped their political strategy, as well as the preferences and constraints of governments in host markets.

7.1 Firm-Driven International Economic Negotiations

This framework of multilateral lobbying also helps us understand the determinants of the plurilateral and sectoral agreements beyond the financial industry that have come to dominate global trade. For example, it can help identify countries, firms, goods, and services of interest in modern trade negotiations such as the Trade in Services Agreement (TiSA),

---

[2] Putnam 1988, p. 459.

CONCLUSION 145

the Environmental Goods Agreement (EGA), and the WTO e-commerce framework. The theory can also offer guidance on a country's negotiating position—not just with regard to the size of its economy, but also its position in the global political economy.

First, it helps explain the cross-industry and cross-country coalitions in TiSA negotiations.[3] TiSA included financial services and at least six other services, including land and air transport, e-commerce, distribution and direct selling, energy and environmental services and telecommunications.[4] It built on and extended the General Agreement on Trade in Services and included new services such as e-commerce and energy and environmental services. The inter-industry linkages brought together a diverse set of industries that tried to shape the new global agreement on trade in services.

Some of the interest groups that were active in the FSA negotiations two decades ago returned to the TiSA negotiations. US insurance industry associations, such as the American Insurance Association and American Council of Life Insurers, issued a joint statement asking TiSA to eliminate barriers in cross-border insurance services. They had similar concerns as in the FSA agreement, including taming state-owned life insurers, such as Japan Post, and removing citizenship requirements for boards of directors.[5] Seven new Internet and technology trade groups called for a ban on data localization.[6] The TiSA negotiations also united the service industry coalitions around the world to create the Global Services Coalition, which framed its support for TiSA by praising the progress made in the negotiations.[7]

Second, in international environment negotiations, the EGA has been a forum of active multilateral lobbying.[8] The negotiations involved

---

[3] The 18 rounds of negotiations among 23 economies (which together account for 70% of global trade in services) started in 2013 (and are currently on hold since President Trump's election in 2016). See Alberto Mucci, "The Most Important Free Trade Agreement You've Never Heard Of," *Politico*, July 7, 2016.

[4] Barbara Matthews, Earl Wayne, and Cecilia Pan, "Trade in Services Agreement: A Way out of the Trade War?," Atlantic Council, July 23, 2018.

[5] Brett Fortnam, "U.S. Insurers' Top TiSA Priorities Are Reinsurance, Data Flows, Equity Caps," *Inside US Trade* 34 (41), October 21, 2016.

[6] These trade groups are the Internet Association, Computer and Communications Industry Association, Information Technology Industry Council, Software Alliance, the App Association, Consumer Technology Association, and Internet Infrastructure Coalition. For more information, see Brett Fortnam, TiSA Tech Letter to U.S. Trade Representative Michael Froman, Oct. 18, 2016. The Information Technology Industry Council (from News Release). https://tinyurl.com/2knzdpjd.

[7] "Services Coalition Calls on TiSA Negotiators to Lock in Progress," *Inside US Trade* 34 (48), December 9, 2016.

[8] The negotiations started at the 2012 Asia-Pacific Economic Cooperation meeting and continued at the WTO until 2016 when the talk collapsed.

18 participants, which represented 46 WTO members including the EU, US, and China, and negotiated tariff reductions on 304 environment-related goods, such as environmental monitoring and analysis, energy efficiency, and waste management.

During the EGA negotiations, firms actively sought to have tariffs removed on specific environmental goods. Firms, in seemingly opposite positions, formed an industry consensus: the US-China business community jointly supported the EGA. The US National Foreign Trade Council and Chinese business associations such as the China Association of Lighting Industry, China Fiberglass and Composites Industry Development Alliance, and Vestas China (wind turbines firm) all supported the agreement.[9] Firms and industry associations also persuaded other countries at the WTO. The International Chamber of Commerce and representatives from MNCs in different industries, such as IKEA, Mercedes-Benz, Ragn-Sells (waste management), and Trashcon (waste management) presented to the WTO group on products and services they would like to be liberalized through a global agreement in the ongoing Trade and Environmental Sustainability Structured Discussions.[10]

Lastly, my theory can also be applied to assess international e-commerce negotiations. The increase in Internet platforms and mobile services highlights the need for new global rules on regulation, interoperable platforms, data security, payment risk management and consumer protection, and access to financial services in e-commerce.[11] The WTO has maintained a work program on e-commerce since 1998.[12] Applying this framework helps us identify major stakeholders like Amazon, eBay, Alibaba, Coupang, and Rakuten, as well as countries where large e-commerce firms are located or want to enter, such as the US, EU, Japan, China, Korea, and India. Since

[9] "While in China, Industry, Academics Push for EGA Conclusion," *Inside US Trade* 34 (42), October 28, 2016.

[10] WTO Trade and Environmental Sustainability Structured Discussions: Informal Working Group on Circular Economy—Circularity Held on 18 May 2022 (10:00-13:00), Summary of discussions, July 14, 2022 (INF/TE/SSD/R/10).

[11] Annual Report of the Committee on Trade in Financial Services to the Council for Trade in Services (2013), October 29, 2013 (S/FIN/28, p. 1).

[12] For example, a working group on trade negotiations on e-commerce, called the Friends of E-Commerce for Development, is composed of Argentina, Chile, Colombia, Costa Rica, Kenya, Mexico, Nigeria, Pakistan, Sri Lanka, and Uruguay. This group held a seminar on Digital Payments and Financial Inclusion in 2017. Since e-commerce is a cross-cutting issue, four WTO bodies have been involved: the Council for Trade in Services, the Council for Trade in Goods, the Council for TRIPS (Trade-Related Aspects of Intellectual Property Rights), and the Committee for Trade and Development.

China's e-commerce business has grown globally, Beijing has increasingly pushed for international cooperation on electronic payment services for cross-border trade in goods and mobile banking.[13] Just as the rise of trade in services necessitated a new international regime, the increase in digital trade will also require a new framework, and MNCs will likely continue to have a growing role in shaping modern trade rules.

As the global reach of firms, through global value chains and technological development, increases to the far corners of the world, firms' multilateral lobbying and industry coalition formation would also increase. Governments and firms will continue to vie for control over regulations to ensure any new frameworks or agreements align with their preferences.

---

[13] Annual Report of the Committee on Trade in Financial Services to the Council for Trade in Services, November 16, 2017, S/FIN/32, p. 1; Annual Report of the Committee on Trade in Financial Services to the Council for Trade in Services, November 28, 2014, S/FIN/29, p. 1.

Bibliography

Abbott, K. W., and D. Snidal (1998, Feb). Why states act through formal international organizations. *Journal of Conflict Resolution 42*(1), 3–32.

Abiad, A., E. Detragiache, and T. Tressel (2010). A new database of financial reforms. *IMF Staff Papers 57*(2), 281–302.

Abiad, A., and A. Mody (2005). Financial reform: What shakes it? What shapes it? *American Economic Review 95*(1), 66–88.

Abraham, F., and S. L. Schmukler (2018). Financial globalization: A glass half empty? In *Handbook of Finance and Development*. Edward Elgar.

Acemoglu, D., V. M. Carvalho, A. Ozdaglar, and A. Tahbaz-Salehi (2012). The network origins of aggregate fluctuations. *Econometrica 80*(5), 1977–2016.

Acemoglu, D., S. Naidu, P. Restrepo, and J. A. Robinson (2019). Democracy does cause growth. *Journal of Political Economy 127*(1), 47–100.

Aggarwal, V. K. (1985). *Liberal protectionism: The international politics of organized textile trade*. Univ of California Press.

Aggarwal, V. K. (1992). The political economy of service sector negotiations in the Uruguay Round. *Fletcher Forum of World Affairs 16*(1), 35–54.

Aggarwal, V. K. (1998). *Institutional designs for a complex world: Bargaining, linkages, and nesting*. Cornell University Press.

Aggarwal, V. K., and S. J. Evenett (2012). Industrial policy choice during the crisis era. *Oxford Review of Economic Policy 28*(2), 261–283.

Aggarwal, V. K., and M. G. Koo (2005). Beyond network power? The dynamics of formal economic integration in Northeast Asia. *Pacific Review 18*(2), 189–216.

Aggarwal, V. K., and J. Ravenhill (2001). Undermining the WTO: The case against "open sectoralism." *AsiaPacific 50*, 1–6.

Ahlquist, J. S. (2006). Economic policy, institutions, and capital flows: Portfolio and direct investment flows in developing countries. *International Studies Quarterly 50*(3), 681–704.

Aitken, B. J., and A. E. Harrison (1999). Do domestic firms benefit from direct foreign investment? Evidence from Venezuela. *American Economic Review 89*(3), 605–618.

Aizenman, J., and I. Noy (2009). Endogenous financial and trade openness. *Review of Development Economics 13*(2), 175–189.

Alfaro, L., A. Chanda, S. Kalemli-Ozcan, and S. Sayek (2010). Does foreign direct investment promote growth? Exploring the role of financial markets on linkages. *Journal of Development Economics 91*(2), 242–256.

Amsden, A. H. (1992). *Asia's next giant: South Korea and late industrialization*. Oxford University Press on Demand.

Andrews, D. M. (1994). Capital mobility and state autonomy: Toward a structural theory of international monetary relations. *International Studies Quarterly 38*(2), 193–218.

Andrianova, S., P. Demetriades, and A. Shortland (2008). Government ownership of banks, institutions, and financial development. *Journal of Development Economics 85*(1–2), 218–252.

Anginer, D., A. C. Bertay, R. Cull, A. Demirgüç-Kunt, and D. S. Mare (2019). Bank regulation and supervision ten years after the global financial crisis. World Bank Policy Research Working Paper 9044.

150 BIBLIOGRAPHY

Aronson, J. D., and G. Feketekuty (1991). *Negotiating to launch negotiations: Getting trade in services onto the GATT agenda*. Pew Diplomatic Training Project, School of International Relations.

Asmundson, I. (2011). Back to basics: What are financial services?: How consumers and businesses acquire financial goods such as loans and insurance. *Finance and Development* 48(1), 46–47.

Austin, G., and C. U. Uche (2007). Collusion and competition in colonial economies: Banking in British West Africa, 1916–1960. *Business History Review* 81(1), 1–26.

Baccini, L., G. Impullitti, and E. J. Malesky (2019). Globalization and state capitalism: Assessing Vietnam's accession to the WTO. *Journal of International Economics* 119, 75–92.

Baccini, L., I. Osgood, and S. Weymouth (2019). The service economy: US trade coalitions in an era of deindustrialization. *Review of International Organizations* 14(2), 261–296.

Baier, S. L., and J. H. Bergstrand (2007). Do free trade agreements actually increase members' international trade? *Journal of International Economics* 71(1), 72–95.

Baker, A. (2005). Who wants to globalize? Consumer tastes and labor markets in a theory of trade policy beliefs. *American Journal of Political Science* 49(4), 924–938.

Balassa, B. (1965). Trade liberalisation and revealed comparative advantage. *The Manchester School* 33(2), 99–123.

Bartel, A. P., and A. E. Harrison (2005). Ownership versus environment: Disentangling the sources of public-sector inefficiency. *Review of Economics and Statistics* 87(1), 135–147.

Bartelme, D., and Y. Gorodnichenko (2015). Linkages and economic development. National Bureau of Economic Research Working Paper 21251.

Barth, J. R., G. Caprio, and R. Levine (2001). *The regulation and supervision of banks around the world: A new database*. Policy Research Working Paper 2588. World Bank Publications.

Baudino, P., and H. Yun (2017). Resolution of non-performing loans—policy options. *FSI Insights on policy implementation*, no. 3.

Baumol, W. J., R. E. Litan, and C. J. Schramm (2007). *Good capitalism, bad capitalism, and the economics of growth and prosperity*. Yale University Press.

Bearce, D. H., and S. Bondanella (2007). Intergovernmental organizations, socialization, and member-state interest convergence. *International Organization* 61(4), 703–733.

Beck, T. (2002). Financial development and international trade: Is there a link? *Journal of International Economics* 57(1), 107–131.

Bekaert, G., C. R. Harvey, and C. Lundblad (2011). Financial openness and productivity. *World Development* 39(1), 1–19.

Berger, A. N., I. Hasan, and M. Zhou (2009). Bank ownership and efficiency in China: What will happen in the world's largest nation? *Journal of Banking & Finance* 33(1), 113–130.

Bernard, A. B., J. B. Jensen, S. J. Redding, and P. K. Schott (2018). Global firms. *Journal of Economic Literature* 56(2), 565–619.

Biglaiser, G., and D. S. Brown (2005). The determinants of economic liberalization in Latin America. *Political Research Quarterly* 58(4), 671–680.

Biglaiser, G., and K. DeRouen Jr. (2007). Following the flag: Troop deployment and US foreign direct investment. *International Studies Quarterly* 51(4), 835–854.

Bliss, H., and B. Russett (1998). Democratic trading partners: The liberal connection, 1962–1989. *Journal of Politics* 60(4), 1126–1147.

Boddewyn, J. J., M. B. Halbrich, and A. C. Perry (1986). Service multinationals: Conceptualization, measurement and theory. *Journal of International Business Studies* 17(3), 41–57.

Bordo, M. D., B. Eichengreen, D. A. Irwin, J. Frankel, and A. M. Taylor (1999). Is globalization today really different from globalization a hundred years ago? [with comments and discussion]. In *Brookings Trade Forum*, pp. 1–72.

Borscheid, P., and N. V. Haueter (2012). *World insurance: The evolution of a global risk network*. Oxford University Press.

Bown, C. P., and D. A. Irwin (2016). *The GATT's starting point: Tariff levels circa 1947*. World Bank.

BIBLIOGRAPHY 151

Brainard, S. L., et al. (1997). An empirical assessment of the proximity-concentration trade-off between multinational sales and trade. *American Economic Review 87*(4), 520–544.

Brooks, S. M. (2004). Explaining capital account liberalization in Latin America: A transitional cost approach. *World Politics 56*(3), 389–430.

Buch, C. M. (2000). Why do banks go abroad?—Evidence from German data. *Financial Markets, Institutions & Instruments 9*(1), 33–67.

Budina, N., H. Garretsen, and d. E. Jong (1999). *Liquidity constraints and investment in transition economies: The case of Bulgaria*. World Bank.

Busch, M. L. (2007). Overlapping institutions, forum shopping, and dispute settlement in international trade. *International Organization 61*(4), 735–761.

Büthe, T., and H. V. Milner (2008). The politics of foreign direct investment into developing countries: Increasing FDI through international trade agreements? *American Journal of Political Science 52*(4), 741–762.

Caprio, G., J. L. Fiechter, R. E. Litan, and M. Pomerleano (2010). *The future of state-owned financial institutions*. Brookings Institution Press.

Central Intelligence Agency (1982). France: Mitterrand's nationalization plans in perspective. A research paper.

Cetorelli, N., and P. E. Strahan (2006). Finance as a barrier to entry: Bank competition and industry structure in local US markets. *Journal of Finance 61*(1), 437–461.

Chaudoin, S., J. Hays, and R. Hicks (2018). Do we really know the WTO cures cancer? *British Journal of Political Science 48*(4), 903–928.

Chinn, M. D., and H. Ito (2006). What matters for financial development? Capital controls, institutions, and interactions. *Journal of Development Economics 81*(1), 163–192.

Chinn, M. D., and H. Ito (2008). A new measure of financial openness. *Journal of Comparative Policy Analysis 10*(3), 309–322.

Cho, Y. J. (1999). *Rising to the Challenge in Asia: A Study of Financial Markets*, Vol. 35, *The banking system of the People's Republic of China*.

Chwieroth, J. (2007). Neoliberal economists and capital account liberalization in emerging markets. *International Organization 61*(2), 443–463.

Claessens, S. (2006). Access to financial services: A review of the issues and public policy objectives. *World Bank Research Observer 21*(2), 207–240.

Claessens, S., A. Demirgüç-Kunt, and H. Huizinga (2001). How does foreign entry affect domestic banking markets? *Journal of Banking & Finance 25*(5), 891–911.

Claessens, S., and E. Perotti (2007). Finance and inequality: Channels and evidence. *Journal of Comparative Economics 35*(4), 748–773.

Clarke, G. R., and R. Cull (2002). Political and economic determinants of the likelihood of privatizing Argentine public banks. *Journal of Law and Economics 45*(1), 165–197.

Cohen, B. J. (1996). Phoenix risen: The resurrection of global finance. *World Politics 48*(2), 268–296.

Congressional Budget Office (2020). *Effects of Recapitalizing Fannie Mae and Freddie Mac Through Administrative Actions*. Publication 56496. Congressional Budget Office.

Cope, R. L. (1987). Local imperatives and imperial policy: The sources of Lord Carnarvon's South African confederation policy. *International Journal of African Historical Studies 20*(4), 601–626.

Cornett, M. M., L. Guo, S. Khaksari, and H. Tehranian (2010). The impact of state ownership on performance differences in privately-owned versus state-owned banks: An international comparison. *Journal of Financial Intermediation 19*(1), 74–94.

Cortell, A. P., and J. W. Davis (1996). How do international institutions matter? The domestic impact of international rules and norms. *International Studies Quarterly 40*(4), 451–478.

Cruz, C., P. Keefer, and C. Scartascini (2018). Database of political institutions 2017. Inter-American Development Bank. Numbers for Development 10, 0001027.

152 BIBLIOGRAPHY

Culpepper, P. D. (2010). *Quiet politics and business power: Corporate control in Europe and Japan.* Cambridge University Press.

Danzman, S. B. (2019). *Merging interests: When domestic firms shape FDI policy.* Cambridge University Press.

Davis, C. L. (2004). International institutions and issue linkage: Building support for agricultural trade liberalization. *American Political Science Review 98*(1), 153–169.

De Figueiredo, J. M., and B. K. Richter (2014). Advancing the empirical research on lobbying. *Annual Review of Political Science 17*, 163–185.

Deardorff, A. V. (2001). International provision of trade services, trade, and fragmentation. *Review of International Economics 9*(2), 233–248.

Díaz-Mora, C., R. Gandoy, and B. González-Díaz (2018). Looking into global value chains: Influence of foreign services on export performance. *Review of World Economics 154*(4), 785–814.

Diebold, F. X., and K. Yılmaz (2015). *Financial and macroeconomic connectedness: A network approach to measurement and monitoring.* Oxford University Press.

Dinç, I. S. (2005). Politicians and banks: Political influences on government-owned banks in emerging markets. *Journal of Financial Economics 77*(2), 453–479.

Dobson, W., and P. Jacquet (1998). *Financial services liberalization in the World Trade Organization.* Peterson Institute for International Economics.

Dorussen, H., E. A. Gartzke, and O. Westerwinter (2016). Networked international politics: Complex interdependence and the diffusion of conflict and peace. *Journal of Peace Research 53*(3), 283–291.

Downs, G. W., D. M. Rocke, and P. N. Barsoom (1996). Is the good news about compliance good news about cooperation? *International Organization 50*(3), 379–406.

Drake, W. J., and K. Nicolaidis (1992). Ideas, interests, and institutionalization: "Trade in services" and the Uruguay Round. *International Organization 46*(1), 37–100.

Drezner, D. W. (2001). Globalization and policy convergence. *International Studies Review 3*(1), 53–78.

Drezner, D. W. (2008). *All politics is global: Explaining international regulatory regimes.* Princeton University Press.

Dunning, J. H. (1980). Toward an eclectic theory of international production: Some empirical tests. *Journal of International Business Studies 11*(1), 9–31.

Dunning, J. H., and S. M. Lundan (2008). *Multinational enterprises and the global economy.* Edward Elgar.

Dür, A., L. Baccini, and M. Elsig (2014). The design of international trade agreements: Introducing a new dataset. *Review of International Organizations 9*(3), 353–375.

Eichengreen, B. (2019). *Globalizing capital: A history of the international monetary system.* Princeton University Press.

Eichengreen, B., and P. Gupta (2011). The two waves of service-sector growth. *Oxford Economic Papers 65*(1), 96–123.

Eichengreen, B., and D. Leblang (2008). Democracy and globalization. *Economics & Politics 20*(3), 289–334.

Elliott, D. J., and K. Yan (2013). *The Chinese financial system: An introduction and overview.* Brookings Institution.

Epstein, R. A. (2017). *Banking on markets: The transformation of bank-state ties in Europe and beyond.* Oxford University Press.

Faccio, M. (2006). Politically connected firms. *American Economic Review 96*(1), 369–386.

Fadinger, H., C. Ghiglino, M. Teteryatnikova, et al. (2015). Productivity, networks and input-output structure. In *2015 Meeting Papers*, Number 624. Society for Economic Dynamics.

Fang, H., and X. Xu (2023). *Chinese insurance markets: Developments and prospects.* Technical report, National Bureau of Economic Research.

Feketekuty, G. (1988). *International trade in services: An overview and blueprint for negotiations.* Ballinger.

Feng, B., and M. K. Nyaw (2010). *Enriching lives: A history of insurance in Hong Kong, 1841–2010*. Hong Kong University Press.

Forbes (2019). Understanding the impact of Deutsche Bank's ill-fated postbank acquisition. *Forbes*, September 19.

Francois, J. (1990). Producer services, scale, and the division of labor. *Oxford Economic Papers 42*(4), 715–729.

Francois, J., and B. Hoekman (2010). Services trade and policy. *Journal of Economic Literature 48*(3), 642–92.

Francois, J., O. Pindyuk, J. Woerz, et al. (2009). *Trends in international trade and FDI in services: A global database of services trade*. Technical report, Institue for International and Development Economics.

Freeman, H. (1998). The role of constituents in US policy development towards trade in financial services. In A. V. Deardorff and R. M. Stern (Eds.), *Constituent interests and US trade policies*, 183. University of Michigan Press.

Freeman, H. (2000). Comments and discussion on financial services and the GATS 2000 round. *Brookings-Wharton Papers on Financial Services 2000*, 455–461.

Frieden, J. A. (1987). *Banking on the world: The politics of American international finance*. Harper & Row.

Frieden, J. A. (1991a). *Debt, development, and democracy: Modern political economy and Latin America, 1965–1985*. Princeton University Press.

Frieden, J. A. (1991b). Invested interests: The politics of national economic policies in a world of global finance. *International Organization 45*(4), 425–451.

Gabaix, X. (2011). The granular origins of aggregate fluctuations. *Econometrica 79*(3), 733–772.

Gale Group (2011). *Gale Encyclopedia of Global Industries*. Gale.

Garrett, G. (1998). *Partisan politics in the global economy*. Cambridge University Press.

Gawande, B. K., P. Krishna, and M. Olarreaga (2012). Lobbying competition over trade policy. *International Economic Review 53*(1), 115–132.

Gawande, K., P. Krishna, and M. J. Robbins (2006). Foreign lobbies and US trade policy. *Review of Economics and Statistics 88*(3), 563–571.

Geishecker, I., and H. Görg (2013). Services offshoring and wages: Evidence from micro data. *Oxford Economic Papers 65*(1), 124–146.

Gereffi, G. (2014). Global value chains in a post-Washington Consensus world. *Review of International Political Economy 21*(1), 9–37.

Gerschenkron, A. (1962). *Economic backwardness in historical perspective: A book of essays*. Technical report. Belknap Press of Harvard University Press.

Goldberg, L. G., and G. A. Hanweck (1991). The growth of the world's 300 largest banking organizations by country. *Journal of Banking & Finance 15*(1), 207–223.

Goldberg, L. G., and D. Johnson (1990). The determinants of US banking activity abroad. *Journal of International Money and Finance 9*(2), 123–137.

Goldstein, J. L., D. Rivers, and M. Tomz (2007). Institutions in international relations: Understanding the effects of the GATT and the WTO on world trade. *International Organization 61*(1), 37–67.

Government Accounting Office (2019). *Report to congressional addressees: Housing finance—prolonged conservatorships of Fannie Mae and Freddie Mac prompt need for reform*.

Gowa, J. (1995). *Allies, adversaries, and international trade*. Princeton University Press.

Grandori, A., and G. Soda (1995). Inter-firm networks: Antecedents, mechanisms and forms. *Organization Studies 16*(2), 183–214.

Gray, J. M., and H. P. Gray (1981). The multinational bank: A financial mnc? *Journal of Banking & Finance 5*(1), 33–63.

Greenberg, M. R. (2003). Opening markets in a turbulent world. *Georgetown Journal of International Affairs* (Summer/Fall), 149–154.

Greenberg, M. R., and L. A. Cunningham (2013). *The AIG story*. John Wiley & Sons.

154 BIBLIOGRAPHY

Grittersová, J., and M. C. Mahutga (2020). Government ownership of banks, political system transparency, and regulatory barriers to new firm entry. *Journal of International Relations and Development, 23*, 781–813.

Grossman, G. M., and E. Helpman (1994). Protection for sale. *American Economie Review 84*(4), 833–850.

Gulotty, R. (2020). *Narrowing the channel: The politics of regulatory protection in international trade.* University of Chicago Press.

Haas, E. B. (1980). Why collaborate? Issue-linkage and international regimes. *World Politics 32*(3), 357–405.

Haber, S. H., D. C. North, and B. R. Weingast (2008). *Political institutions and financial development.* Stanford University Press.

Haggard, S., (1990). *Pathways from the periphery: The politics of growth in the newly industrializing countries.* Cornell University Press.

Haggard, S., and S. Maxfield (1996). The political economy of financial internationalization in the developing world. *International Organization 50*(1), 35–68.

Hansen, B. B. (2004). Full matching in an observational study of coaching for the SAT. *Journal of the American Statistical Association 99*(467), 609–618.

Hathaway, O. A. (2007). Why do countries commit to human rights treaties? *Journal of Conflict Resolution 51*(4), 588–621.

Hau, H., and M. Thum (2009). Subprime crisis and board (in-)competence: Private versus public banks in Germany. *Economic Policy 24*(60), 701–752.

Helpman, E., M. J. Melitz, and S. R. Yeaple (2004). Export versus FDI with heterogeneous firms. *American Economic Review 94*(1), 300–316.

Hendrickson, J. M. (2001). The long and bumpy road to Glass-Steagall reform: A historical and evolutionary analysis of banking legislation. *American Journal of Economics and Sociology 60*(4), 849–879.

Hijzen, A., M. Pisu, R. Upward, and P. W. Wright (2011). Employment, job turnover, and trade in producer services: UK firm-level evidence. *Canadian Journal of Economics/Revue canadienne d'économique 44*(3), 1020–1043.

Hirschman, A. O. (1958). *The strategy of economic development.* Yale University Press.

Ho, D. E., K. Imai, G. King, and E. A. Stuart (2007). Matching as nonparametric preprocessing for reducing model dependence in parametric causal inference. *Political Analysis 15*(3), 199–236.

Hoekman, B., A. Mattoo, and A. Sapir (2007). The political economy of services trade liberalization: A case for international regulatory cooperation? *Oxford Review of Economic Policy 23*(3), 367–391.

Hoekman, B., and B. Shepherd (2017). Services productivity, trade policy and manufacturing exports. *The World Economy 40*(3), 499–516.

Hoff, P. D., and M. D. Ward (2004). Modeling dependencies in international relations networks. *Political Analysis 12*(2), 160–175.

Hofmann, C., A. Osnago, and M. Ruta (2017). Horizontal depth: A new database on the content of preferential trade agreements. World Bank Policy Research Working Paper 7981.

IMF (2009). *Balance of Payments Manual*, Volume 6. International Monetary Fund.

IMF (2020). International financial statistics. https://tinyurl.com/2rp7n2dh

Inostroza, A. (1979). Nationalization of the banking system in Chile. In S. Sideri (Ed.), *Chile 1970–73: Economic development and its international setting*, pp. 275–312. Springer.

International Business Publications (2015). *Ghana mining laws and regulations handbook*, Volume 1, *Strategic information and basic laws*. International Business Publications.

Javorcik, B. S. (2004). Does foreign direct investment increase the productivity of domestic firms? In search of spillovers through backward linkages. *American Economic Review 94*(3), 605–627.

Jensen, J. B. (2008a). Trade in high-tech services. *Journal of Industry, Competition and Trade 8*(3–4), 181–197.

BIBLIOGRAPHY   155

Jensen, J. B., D. P. Quinn, and S. Weymouth (2015). The influence of firm global supply chains and foreign currency undervaluations on US trade disputes. *International Organization 69*(4), 913–947.

Jensen, N. M. (2004). Crisis, conditions, and capital: The effect of International Monetary Fund agreements on foreign direct investment inflows. *Journal of Conflict Resolution 48*(2), 194–210.

Jensen, N. M. (2008). *Nation-states and the multinational corporation: A political economy of foreign direct investment.* Princeton University Press.

Jensen, N. M., G. Biglaiser, Q. Li, E. Malesky, P. M. Pinto, S. M. Pinto, and J. Staats (2012). *Politics and foreign direct investment.* University of Michigan Press.

Jones, C. I. (2011). Intermediate goods and weak links in the theory of economic development. *American Economic Journal: Macroeconomics 3*(2), 1–28.

Jung, D. F., and D. A. Lake (2011). Markets, hierarchies, and networks: An agent-based organizational ecology. *American Journal of Political Science 55*(4), 972–990.

Katzenstein, P. J., et al. (1978). *Between power and plenty: Foreign economic policies of advanced industrial states.* University of Wisconsin Press.

Kelsey, J. (2008). *Serving whose interests?: The political economy of trade in services agreements.* Routledge-Cavendish.

Keohane, R. O. (1984). *After hegemony: Cooperation and discord in the world political economy.* Princeton University Press.

Keohane, R. O. (2009). The old IPE and the new. *Review of International Political Economy 16*(1), 34–46.

Kerner, A. (2009). Why should I believe you? The costs and consequences of bilateral investment treaties. *International Studies Quarterly 53*(1), 73–102.

Kim, I. S. (2017). Political cleavages within industry: Firm-level lobbying for trade liberalization. *American Political Science Review 111*(1), 1–20.

Kim, I. S., H. V. Milner, T. Bernauer, I. Osgood, G. Spilker, and D. Tingley (2019). Firms and global value chains: Identifying firms' multidimensional trade preferences. *International Studies Quarterly 63*(1), 153–167.

Kim, I. S., and I. Osgood (2018). Firms in trade and trade politics: New insights for the political economy of globalization. *Annual Review of Political Science 22*, 399–417.

Kim, S. Y. (2021). Investment commitments in PTAs and MNCs in partner countries. *Economics & Politics 33*(3), 415–442.

King, R. G., and R. Levine (1993). Finance, entrepreneurship and growth. *Journal of Monetary Economics 32*(3), 513–542.

Kinne, B. J. (2013). Network dynamics and the evolution of international cooperation. *American Political Science Review 107*, 766–785.

Kireyev, M. A. (2002). *Liberalization of trade in financial services and financial sector stability (analytical approach).* Publication 138. International Monetary Fund.

Koenker, R., and K. F. Hallock (2001). Quantile regression. *Journal of Economic Perspectives 15*(4), 143–156.

Konan, D. E., and K. E. Maskus (2006). Quantifying the impact of services liberalization in a developing country. *Journal of Development Economics 81*(1), 142–162.

Kornai, J. (1980). *Economics of shortage. v. ab.*

Kornai, J., E. Maskin, and G. Roland (2003). Understanding the soft budget constraint. *Journal of Economic Literature 41*(4), 1095–1136.

Kose, A., K. Rogoff, E. S. Prasad, and S.-J. Wei (2004). Effects on financial globalization on developing countries: Some empirical evidence. In *Effects on financial globalization on developing countries.* International Monetary Fund. IMF Occasional Paper 220. https://scholar.harvard.edu/sites/scholar.harvard.edu/files/rogoff/files/imf_op220.pdf

Kose, M. A., E. Prasad, K. Rogoff, and S.-J. Wei (2009). Financial globalization: A reappraisal. *IMF Staff Papers 56*(1), 8–62.

156 BIBLIOGRAPHY

Kosmidis, I., and D. Firth (2009). Bias reduction in exponential family nonlinear models. *Biometrika 96*(4), 793–804.

Krasner, S. D. (1976). State power and the structure of international trade. *World Politics 28*(3), 317–347.

Krasner, S. D. (1982). Structural causes and regime consequences: Regimes as intervening variables. *International Organization 36*(2), 185–205.

Krasner, S. D. (1983). *International regimes.* Cornell University Press.

Krueger, A. O. (1974). The political economy of the rent-seeking society. *American Economic Review 64*(3), 291–303.

La Porta, R., and F. Lopez-de Silanes (1999). The benefits of privatization: Evidence from Mexico. *Quarterly Journal of Economics 114*(4), 1193–1242.

La Porta, R., F. Lopez-de Silanes, and A. Shleifer (1999). Corporate ownership around the world. *Journal of Finance 54*(2), 471–517.

La Porta, R., F. Lopez-de Silanes, and A. Shleifer (2002). Government ownership of banks. *Journal of Finance 57*(1), 265–301.

Lake, D. A. (2009). Open economy politics: A critical review. *Review of International Organizations 4*(3), 219–244.

Lardy, N. R. (1998). *China's unfinished economic revolution.* Brookings Institution Press.

Lehmann, P., T. Matthieß, N. Merz, S. Regel, and A. Werner (2017). Manifesto corpus. Version 2017-2. WZB Berlin Social Science Center.

Levine, R. (1997). Financial development and economic growth: Views and agenda. *Journal of Economic Literature 35*(2), 688–726.

Li, Q., and A. Resnick (2003). Reversal of fortunes: Democratic institutions and foreign direct investment inflows to developing countries. *International Organization 57*(1), 175–211.

Lin, J. Y., F. Cai, and Z. Li (1998). Competition, policy burdens, and state-owned enterprise reform. *American Economic Review 88*(2), 422–427.

Lipset, S. M. (1959, March). Some social requisites of democracy: Economic development and political legitimacy. *American Political Science Review 53*(1), 69–105.

Lodefalk, M. (2014). The role of services for manufacturing firm exports. *Review of World Economics 150*(1), 59–82.

Lohmann, S. (1997). Linkage politics. *Journal of Conflict Resolution 41*(1), 38–67.

Lopez-de Silanes, F., and G. Zamarripa (1995). Deregulation and privatization of commercial banking. *Revista de Análisis Económico–Economic Analysis Review 10*(2), 113–164.

Lu, D., S. M. Thangavelu, and Q. Hu (2005). Biased lending and non-performing loans in China's banking sector. *Journal of Development Studies 41*(6), 1071–1091.

MacDonald, P. K. (2018). Embedded authority: A relational network approach to hierarchy in world politics. *Review of International Studies 44*(1), 128–150.

Madeira, M. A. (2016). New trade, new politics: Intra-industry trade and domestic political coalitions. *Review of International Political Economy 23*(4), 677–711.

Malesky, E. J. (2009). Foreign direct investors as agents of economic transition: An instrumental variables analysis. *Quarterly Journal of Political Science 4*(1), 59–85.

Malesky, E. J., and H. V. Milner (2021). Fostering global value chains through international agreements: Evidence from Vietnam. *Economics & Politics 33*(3), 443–482.

Malesky, E. J., and M. Taussig (2009). Where is credit due? Legal institutions, connections, and the efficiency of bank lending in Vietnam. *Journal of Law, Economics, & Organization 25*(2), 535–578.

Manning, C., H. Aswicahyono, et al. (2012). *Trade and employment in services: The case of indonesia.* Technical report, International Labour Organization.

Manova, K. (2013). Credit constraints, heterogeneous firms, and international trade. *Review of Economic Studies 80*(2), 711–744.

Mansfield, E. D. (1995). *Power, trade, and war.* Princeton University Press.

Mansfield, E. D., H. V. Milner, and B. P. Rosendorff (2002). Why democracies cooperate more: Electoral control and international trade agreements. *International Organization 56*(3), 477–513.

BIBLIOGRAPHY   157

Mansfield, E. D. and E. Reinhardt (2003). Multilateral determinants of regionalism: The effects of GATT/WTO on the formation of preferential trading arrangements. *International Organization* 57(4), 829–862.

Marchetti, J. A., and P. C. Mavroidis (2011). The genesis of the GATS (General Agreement on Trade in Services). *European Journal of International Law* 22(3), 689–721.

Markusen, J. R. (1989). Trade in producer services and in other specialized intermediate inputs. *American Economic Review* 79(1), 85–95.

Martin, R. (2011). *Services commitments in preferential trade agreements: An expanded dataset.* Technical report, WTO Staff Working Paper ERSD-2011-18.

Martinez-Diaz, L. (2009). *Globalizing in hard times: The politics of banking-sector opening in the emerging world.* Cornell University Press.

Maskin, E. S. (1996). Theories of the soft budget-constraint. *Japan and the World Economy* 8(2), 125–133.

Mattoo, A. (1999). *Financial services and the World Trade Organization: Liberalization commitments of the developing and transition economies.* Policy Research Working Paper 2184. World Bank Publications.

Mayda, A. M., and D. Rodrik (2005). Why are some people (and countries) more protectionist than others? *European Economic Review* 49(6), 1393–1430.

McKinnon, R. I. (1982). The order of economic liberalization: Lessons from Chile and Argentina. In *Carnegie-Rochester Conference Series on Public Policy*, Volume 17, pp. 159–186. Elsevier.

McNally, C. A. (2002). China's state-owned enterprises: Thriving or crumbling? *Asia-Pacific Issues* 59, 1.

Megginson, W. L., and J. M. Netter (2001). From state to market: A survey of empirical studies on privatization. *Journal of Economic Literature* 39(2), 321–389.

Melitz, M. (2003). The impact of trade on aggregate industry productivity and intra-industry reallocations. *Econometrica* 71(6), 1695–1725.

Melvin, J. R. (1989). Trade in producer services: A Heckscher-Ohlin approach. *Journal of Political Economy* 97(5), 1180–1196.

Menaldo, V., and D. Yoo (2015). Democracy, elite bias, and financial development in Latin America. *World Politics* 67, 726–759.

Mertens, D., and M. Thiemann (2018). Market-based but state-led: The role of public development banks in shaping market-based finance in the European Union. *Competition & Change* 22(2), 184–204.

Micco, A., U. Panizza, and M. Yanez (2007). Bank ownership and performance: Does politics matter? *Journal of Banking & Finance* 31(1), 219–241.

Milner, H. V. (1988a). *Resisting protectionism: Global industries and the politics of international trade.* Princeton University Press.

Milner, H. V. (1988b). Trading places: Industries for free trade. *World Politics* 40(3), 350–376.

Milner, H. V. (1992). International theories of cooperation among nations: Strengths and weaknesses. *World Politics* 44(3), 466–496.

Milner, H. V., and B. Judkins (2004). Partisanship, trade policy, and globalization: Is there a left-right divide on trade policy? *International Studies Quarterly* 48(1), 95–119.

Milner, H. V., and K. Kubota (2005). Why the move to free trade? Democracy and trade policy in the developing countries. *International Organization* 59(1), 107–143.

Milner, H. V., and B. Mukherjee (2009). Democratization and economic globalization. *Annual Review of Political Science* 12, 163–181.

Milner, H. V., and D. B. Yoffie (1989). Between free trade and protectionism: Strategic trade policy and a theory of corporate trade demands. *International Organization* 43(2), 239–272.

Miroudot, S., and C. Cadestin (2017). Services in global value chains: From inputs to value-creating activities. OECD Trade Policy Papers No. 197. OECD Publishing.

Miroudot, S., J. Sauvage, and B. Shepherd (2012). Trade costs and productivity in services sectors. *Economics Letters* 114(1), 36–38.

158 BIBLIOGRAPHY

Mosley, L. (2003). *Global capital and national governments.* Cambridge University Press.

Mosley, L. (2013). *Interview research in political science.* Cornell University Press.

Mosley, L., and D. A. Singer (2008). Taking stock seriously: Equity-market performance, government policy, and financial globalization. *International Studies Quarterly 52*(2), 405–425.

Mukherjee, B., and D. A. Singer (2010). International institutions and domestic compensation: The IMF and the politics of capital account liberalization. *American Journal of Political Science 54*(1), 45–60.

Musacchio, A., A. M. Farias, and S. G. Lazzarini (2014). *Reinventing state capitalism.* Harvard University Press.

Naqvi, N., A. Henow, and H.-J. Chang (2018). Kicking away the financial ladder? German development banking under economic globalisation. *Review of International Political Economy 25*(5), 672–698.

Narlikar, A. (2003). *International trade and developing countries: Bargaining coalitions in the GATT & WTO.* Taylor & Francis.

Nigh, D., K. R. Cho, and S. Krishnan (1986). The role of location-related factors in US banking involvement abroad: An empirical examination. *Journal of International Business Studies 17*(3), 59–72.

Oatley, T. (2011). The reductionist gamble: Open economy politics in the global economy. *International Organization 65*(2), 311–341.

Oatley, T. (2017). Open economy politics and trade policy. *Review of International Political Economy*, 1–19.

Oatley, T., W. K. Winecoff, A. Pennock, and S. B. Danzman (2013). The political economy of global finance: A network model. *Perspectives on Politics 11*(1), 133–153.

OECD (2018). *Ownership and governance of state-owned enterprises: A compendium of national practices.* OECD.

O'Rourke, K. H. and R. Sinnott (2006). The determinants of individual attitudes towards immigration. *European Journal of Political Economy 22*(4), 838–861.

Osgood, I. (2018). Globalizing the supply chain: Firm and industrial support for us trade agreements. *International Organization 72*(2), 455–484.

Osgood, I. (2021). Vanguards of globalization: Organization and political action among America's pro-trade firms. *Business and Politics 23*(1), 1–35.

Osgood, I., D. Tingley, T. Bernauer, I. S. Kim, H. V. Milner, and G. Spilker (2017). The charmed life of superstar exporters: Survey evidence on firms and trade policy. *Journal of Politics 79*(1), 133–152.

Pandya, S. S. (2014). *Trading spaces.* Cambridge University Press.

Paulson, H. (2015). *Dealing with China.* Hachette UK.

Pepinsky, T. B. (2012). Do currency crises cause capital account liberalization? *International Studies Quarterly 56*(3), 544–559.

Pepinsky, T. B. (2013). The domestic politics of financial internationalization in the developing world. *Review of International Political Economy 20*(4), 848–880.

Peters, M. (2017). *Trading barriers: Immigration and the remaking of globalization.* Princeton University Press.

Pigou, A. C. (1924). *The Economics of Welfare.* Macmillan.

Pinto, P. M. (2013). *Partisan investment in the global economy: Why the left loves foreign direct investment and FDI loves the left.* Cambridge University Press.

Pinto, P. M., and S. M. Pinto (2008). The politics of investment partisanship: And the sectoral allocation of foreign direct investment. *Economics & Politics 20*(2), 216–254.

Pollins, B. M. (1989). Does trade still follow the flag? *American Political Science Review 83*(2), 465–480.

Pond, A. (2018). Financial liberalization: Stable autocracies and constrained democracies. *Comparative Political Studies 51*(1), 105–135.

Przeworski, A., M. E. Alvarez, J. A. C. Cheibub, and F. Limongi (2000). *Democracy and development: Political institutions and well-being in the world, 1950–1990.* Cambridge University Press.

BIBLIOGRAPHY 159

Przeworski, A., and J. R. Vreeland (2000). The effect of IMF programs on economic growth. *Journal of Development Economics 62*(2), 385–421.

Putnam, R. D. (1988). Diplomacy and domestic politics: The logic of two-level games. *International Organization 42*(3), 427–460.

Quinn, D. P. (2000). Political and international financial liberalization. Paper presented at the 2000 meeting of the American Political Science Association. McDonough School of Business, Georgetown University.

Quinn, D. P. (2003). Capital account liberalization and financial globalization, 1890–1999: A synoptic view. *International Journal of Finance & Economics 8*(3), 189–204.

Quinn, D. P., and C. Inclan (1997). The origins of financial openness: A study of current and capital account liberalization. *American Journal of Political Science 41*(3), 771–813.

Quinn, D. P., and A. M. Toyoda (2007). Ideology and voter preferences as determinants of financial globalization. *American Journal of Political Science 51*(2), 344–363.

Quinn, D. P., and A. M. Toyoda (2008). Does capital account liberalization lead to growth? *Review of Financial Studies 21*(3), 1403–1449.

Rajan, R. G., and L. Zingales (2003). The great reversals: The politics of financial development in the twentieth century. *Journal of Financial Economics 69*(1), 5–50.

Reisenbichler, A. (2015). The domestic sources and power dynamics of regulatory networks: Evidence from the Financial Stability Forum. *Review of International Political Economy 22*(5), 996–1024.

Rodriguez-Clare, A. (1996). Multinationals, linkages, and economic development. *American Economic Review 86*(4), 852–873.

Rodrik, D. (1995). Getting interventions right: How South Korea and Taiwan grew rich. *Economic Policy 10*(20), 53–107.

Roland, G. (2000). *Transition and economics: Politics, markets, and firms.* MIT press.

Rose, A. K. (2004). Do we really know that the WTO increases trade? *American Economic Review 94*(1), 98–114.

Rosendorff, B. P., and H. V. Milner (2001). The optimal design of international trade institutions: Uncertainty and escape. *International Organization 55*(4), 829–857.

Rowthorn, R., and R. Ramaswamy (1999). Growth, trade, and deindustrialization. *IMF Staff Papers 46*(1), 18–41.

Rudra, N. (2005). Globalization and the strengthening of democracy in the developing world. *American Journal of Political Science 49*(4), 704–730.

Ruggie, J. G. (1982). International regimes, transactions, and change: Embedded liberalism in the postwar economic order. *International Organization 36*(2), 379–415.

Sauvant, K. P. (1993). The tradability of services. International Corporations in Services, United Nations Library on Transnational Corporations, London, 300–315.

Schattschneider, E. E. (1935). *Politics, pressures and the tariff: A study of free private enterprise in pressure politics, as shown in the 1929–1930 revision of the tariff.* Prentice-Hall.

Scheve, K., and M. J. Slaughter (2001). What determines individual trade-policy preferences? *Journal of International Economics 54*(2), 267–292.

Scheve, K., and M. J. Slaughter (2004). Economic insecurity and the globalization of production. *American Journal of Political Science 48*(4), 662–674.

Sekhon, J. S. (2009). Opiates for the matches: Matching methods for causal inference. *Annual Review of Political Science 12*, 487–508.

Senate Committee on Homeland Security and Governmental Affairs (2005). Securing American Sovereignty: A Review of the United States' Relationship with the WTO. Hearing before the Federal Financial Management, Government Information, and International Security Subcommittee. 109th Cong. 1st sess. 15 July.

Sherman, L. B. (1998). Wildly enthusiastic about the first multilateral agreement on trade in telecommunications services. Federal Communications Law Journal *51*, 61.

Shleifer, A., and R. W. Vishny (1994). Politicians and firms. *Quarterly Journal of Economics 109*(4), 995–1025.

160 BIBLIOGRAPHY

Shleifer, A., and R. W. Vishny (1997). A survey of corporate governance. *Journal of Finance* 52(2), 737–783.

Shleifer, A., and R. W. Vishny (2002). *The grabbing hand: Government pathologies and their cures.* Harvard University Press.

Simmons, B. A., (2000). International law and state behavior: Commitment and compliance in international monetary affairs. *American Political Science Review* 94(4), 819–835.

Simmons, B. A., and Z. Elkins (2004). The globalization of liberalization: Policy diffusion in the international political economy. *American Political Science Review* 98(1), 171–189.

Sims, J., and J. Romero (2013). Latin American debt crisis of the 1980s. Federal Reserve History 22. https://www.federalreservehistory.org/essays/latin-american-debt-crisis

Steinberg, D. A., S. C. Nelson, and C. Nguyen (2018). Does democracy promote capital account liberalization? *Review of International Political Economy* 25(6), 854–883.

Steinberg, R. H. (2002). In the shadow of law or power? Consensus-based bargaining and outcomes in the GATT/WTO. *International Organization* 56(2), 339–374.

Stigler, G. J. (1971). The theory of economic regulation. *Bell Journal of Economics and Management Science*, 3–21.

Stiglitz, J. E. (1993). The role of the state in financial markets. *World Bank Economic Review* 7(Suppl. 1), 19–52.

Subramanian, A., and S.-J. Wei (2007). The WTO promotes trade, strongly but unevenly. *Journal of International Economics* 72(1), 151–175.

Sykes, J. B. (2018). *Banking law: An overview of federal preemption in the dual banking system.* Congressional Research Service Report R-45081.

Taboada, A. G. (2011). The impact of changes in bank ownership structure on the allocation of capital: International evidence. *Journal of Banking & Finance* 35(10), 2528–2543.

Tamirisa, N. T., P. Sorsa, G. Bannister, B. McDonald, and J. Wieczorek (2000). *Trade Policy in Financial Service.* International Monetary Fund.

Tingley, D., C. Xu, A. Chilton, and H. V. Milner (2015). The political economy of inward FDI: Opposition to Chinese mergers and acquisitions. *Chinese Journal of International Politics* 8(1), 27–57.

Tomz, M., J. L. Goldstein, and D. Rivers (2007). Do we really know that the WTO increases trade? Comment. *American Economic Review* 97(5), 2005–2018.

US Department of State (2019). 2019 Investment Climate Statements: Japan.

US Department of the Treasury (1998). National Treatment Study 1998.

US House of Representatives. Committee on Ways and Means, Subcommittee on Trade (1999, March 4). Hearing on the Importance of Trade Negotiations–in Fighting Foreign Protectionism: Active US Involvement, 106th Cong.

USITC (1998). *The year in trade: Operation of the Trade Agreements Program during 1997.* USITC 49th Report 3103, Volume 49. USITC Publications.

Vastine, J. R. (2005). Services negotiations in the Doha Round: Promise and reality. *Global Economy Journal* 5(4).

Velasco, A. (1991). Liberalization, crisis, intervention: the Chilean financial system, 1975–1985. In *Banking crises: Cases and issues.* International Monetary Fund.

Verdier, D. (2000). The rise and fall of state banking in OECD countries. *Comparative Political Studies* 33(3), 283–318.

Vernon, R. (1971). *Sovereignty at bay: The multinational spread of US enterprises.* Longman.

Von Stein, J. (2005). Do treaties constrain or screen? Selection bias and treaty compliance. *American Political Science Review* 99(4), 611–622.

Wagner, C. Z. (1999). The new WTO agreement on financial services and chapter 14 of NAFTA: Has free trade in banking finally arrived. *NAFTA: Law & Business Review of the Americas 5*, 5.

Walter, S. (2021). The backlash against globalization. *Annual Review of Political Science* 24(1), 421–442.

Ward, M. D., K. Stovel, and A. Sacks (2011). Network analysis and political science. *Annual Review of Political Science* 14, 245–264.

Webster, T. (2013). Paper Compliance: How China implements WTO decisions. *Michigan Journal of International Law 35*, 525.

Wei, S.-J., and T. Wang (1997). The Siamese twins: Do state-owned banks favor state-owned enterprises in China? *China Economic Review 8*(1), 19–29.

Weill, L. (2003). Banking efficiency in transition economies: The role of foreign ownership. *Economics of Transition 11*(3), 569–592.

Wellhausen, R. L. (2014). *The shield of nationality: When governments break contracts with foreign firms*. Cambridge University Press.

Weymouth, S. (2017). Service firms in the politics of US trade policy. *International Studies Quarterly 61*(4), 935–947.

Wirth, D. A. (1997). International trade agreements: Vehicles for regulatory reform. University of Chicago Legal Forum *1999*, Article 11.

Woll, C., and A. Artigas (2007). When trade liberalization turns into regulatory reform: The impact on business-government relations in international trade politics. *Regulation & Governance 1*(2), 121–138.

World Bank (2020). World Development Indicators. World Bank.

WTO (2019). *World trade report: The future of services trade*. WTO.

WTO Singapore Ministerial Meeting: Hearing Before the Subcommittee on Trade of the Committee on Ways and Means, House of Representatives, 105th Cong. 1 (1997) (Statement of Robert Vastine).

Yannopoulos, G. N. (1983). The growth of transnational banking. In Mark Casson (Ed.), *The growth of international business*. Routledge.

Yeung, G. (2021). Chinese state-owned commercial banks in reform: Inefficient and yet credible and functional? *Journal of Chinese Governance 6*(2), 198–231.

You, H. Y. (2023). Dynamic lobbying: Evidence from foreign lobbying in the US Congress. *Economics & Politics 35* (2): 445–469. https://onlinelibrary.wiley.com/doi/full/10.1111/ecpo.12223

Zhang, D., J. Cai, D. G. Dickinson, and A. M. Kutan (2016). Non-performing loans, moral hazard and regulation of the Chinese commercial banking system. *Journal of Banking & Finance 63*, 48–60.

Index

AIG 8, 31, 114
  China 112, 124
  East Asia 32
  Japan 32, 103
  Malaysia 38, 105
American Express 8, 32
  China 122

Bank for International Settlements 9, 36, 124
Barshefsky, Charlene 37
Blackrock
  China 121
Bloomberg 121
Bush, George W. 119

capital account liberalization 5, 43, 124
China
  Banking and Insurance Regulatory
    Commission 119
  China Banking Regulatory
    Commission 119
  China Insurance Regulatory
    Commission 119
  Cultural Revolution 112
  financial linkage 113
  financial regulators 119
  FSA
    geographic liberalization 116
    restrictions 116
    schedule 117
  insurance 114
  People's Bank of China 112
  People's Insurance Company of China 112
  Permanent Normal Trading Relations 114
  regulatory reform 111
  Securities Regulatory Commission 119
  SOE 112
  SOFI 113
  State Council 116
  WTO 114
    dispute settlement mechanism 121
Citibank 8, 32, 55
  Africa 57
  Belgium 54

China 119
East Asia 127
Gabon 59
Ghana 57
Kenya 59
Latin America 128
Nigeria 53, 59
Zambia 59
Coalition of Services Industries (CSI) 32, 120

D'Amato, Alfonse 37
Dow 121

e-commerce 146
Environmental Goods Agreement (EGA) 145

Fidelity
  China 121
financial
  crisis 67, 74, 87, 93, 97
  entry regulations 75, 80, 117
  globalization 3, 17
  liberalization 3
  linkage 19, 50, 113
    measure 48
    US 50
    world 61
  regulations 98
    international depository 98
  regulators
    Capital Market Board 96
    Insurance Supervisory Authority 96
    Ministry of Finance 96
    Securities and Exchange Board 96
    Securities Commission 96
    Superintendent of Insurance 96
  trade restrictions 14, 79
Financial Leaders Group (FLG) 34
Financial Services Agreement (FSA)
  17, 70, 98
foreign banks
  East Asia 127
  Latin America 129
Foreign Direct Investment (FDI) 136

164 INDEX

GATS 4, 36
General Agreement on Trade in Services,
  see GATS
Ghana
  Citibank 57
  cocoa 57
  Eurobonds 58
  gold 57
  oil 57
Glass-Steagall Act 108
government ownership 3, 70

Hu, Jintao 119

IMF 9, 67, 124
independent regulation 91, 98
industry coalition 31

J.P. Morgan 52
  China 120
  East Asia 127
  Latin America 128
Japan
  Financial Services Agency 104
  regulatory reform 104
Jiang, Zemin 114

Korea
  Financial Supervisory Services 104–105
  regulatory reform 104

Malaysia
  AIG 105
  regulatory reform 105
Mastercard
  China 120
mergers and acquisitions 129
multilateral lobbying 7, 18, 144
  mechanism 31
multinational financial corporations (MFC) 2,
      17, 51
  Barclays 33, 54, 130
  BBVA 57, 130
  Credit Suisse 128, 130
  Goldman Sachs 58, 114
  HSBC 52, 102, 128, 130
  ICBC 73, 124
  J.P. Morgan 53, 128, 130
  Mastercard 120
  Morgan Stanley 33, 109, 114
  Santander 57, 128, 130
  Société Générale 128, 130

Standard Chartered 52, 128, 130
  UBS 121, 128, 130
  Visa 120, 122

national treatment 80, 91, 117
network analysis 48

Obama, Barack 111, 119
OECD Input-Output Database 48, 61

Paulson, Hank 114, 119
portfolio investment 133

quiet politics 38

Reed, John S., 32
regulatory reforms
  Argentina 99
  Bolivia 95, 99, 102
  Brazil 61, 78, 88, 99
  Chile 99, 101
  China 111
  Colombia 99, 102
  Costa Rica 101
  Czech Republic 94
  Dominican Republic 99
  East Asia 102
  Eastern Europe 94
  El Salvador 101
  Honduras 101
  Hungary 94
  India 52, 70, 76, 106
  Indonesia 52, 67, 105
  Japan 32, 102, 109
  Korea 67, 76, 95
  Latin America 98
  Malaysia 38, 67, 76, 105
  Mexico 101
  Nicaragua 102
  Peru 101
  Philippines 52, 67, 77
  Poland 94
  Singapore 33, 83, 104
  Slovenia 94
  Southeast Asia 105
  Thailand 61, 67, 76, 87, 105
  US 108
  Venezuela 101
  Vietnam 61, 104, 124
Reuters 121
Robinson III, James D., 32
Rubin, Robert 37

INDEX 165

Socialism with Chinese Characteristics 112
state-owned financial institutions
      (SOFIs) 19, 73
   China 73, 112, 124

tax havens 67
trade in financial services 5, 134
trade in Services 9, 37
Trade in Services Agreement (TiSA)
      144
Trump, Donald 120

Union Pay 120
US Trade Representative (USTR) 32

US-China Strategic and Economic
   Dialogue 119

Visa
   China 120

WTO 4, 47
   Chinese accession 77, 114
   Dispute Settlement Mechanism 121

Xi, Jinping 119
Xinhua 121

Zhu, Rongji 114